quick & easy

korean

cooking

quick & easy
korean
cooking

MORE THAN 70 EVERYDAY RECIPES

BY **CECILIA HAE-JIN LEE**

PHOTOGRAPHS BY **JULIE TOY** AND **CECILIA HAE-JIN LEE**

CHRONICLE BOOKS
SAN FRANCISCO

Library of Congress Cataloging-in-Publication Data available.

ISBN 978-0-8118-6146-5

Manufactured in china

Design and Illustration by design army
Food styling by valerie aikman-smith
Typesetting by design army

10 9 8 7 6 5 4 3 2 1

Chronicle Books LLC
680 Second Street
San Francisco, California 94107
www.chroniclebooks.com

To my husband, Tim, who is my companion,
friend, and ultimate taste tester.

acknowledgments

Like a crowded kitchen alive with preparation for a large celebration, the efforts of many hands and minds help pull a book together. There are numerous people—family, friends, strangers—who have shared their culinary wonders. I thank them for the meals I've enjoyed and the knowledge of food they've shared throughout the years.

I am grateful for my family—my mom Julia Mi-Ja, my dad Daniel Pal-Woo, my sister Catherine Hae-Ran, and my brother Sang. They've shared my love of food, given me a sense of adventure, and supported me through many meals and projects.

A big thank you to everyone at Chronicle Books, who helped create and support the physical book, especially Bill LeBlond for believing in the project, Anne Donnard for her wonderful design, Julie Toy for bringing my recipes alive in pictures, and Amy Treadwell for keeping us on track and pulling it all together.

I have to give a special thanks to my husband, Tim Maloney, whose patience, palate, and editing eye have contributed so much to this project. The kitchen would not be as clean without him and I'm just glad he hasn't left me for his new lover—the dishwasher.

I also wish to thank my family in Korea: my Great Aunt, my Uncle Mangyu, and the family for their unwavering generosity with their home whenever their crazy American niece comes to town. Without my Aunt Younggyu's car and my Aunt Jumi's knowledge and companionship I wouldn't have been able to capture the photos I gathered during my travels. I realize through my large extended family that the food we've shared throughout the generations can be enjoyed for many more to come.

contents

introduction

I don't remember learning how to cook Korean food, just as I don't remember learning how to read. I do remember being too short to reach the counter and having to pull up a chair to the kitchen sink to wash the rice for dinner. Learning how to cook was a gradual process, starting with simple things like peeling potatoes and carrots for my mom and eventually leading to making feasts for dozens of family and friends.

I remember learning English, though, gradually understanding how the letters were formed, how they sounded, and how my mouth felt when saying certain words. Eventually English became so ingrained that I began thinking in it without having to translate it in my mind.

I think learning a new cuisine is very similar to learning a foreign language. You begin with small tastes at first, deciding that you like it and want to learn more about it. You take in more and more, and you gradually become confident enough to try it on your own.

Lucky for you Korean cooking is as easy as (if not easier than) learning the Korean language. Just as you can learn how to read the characters in an afternoon, the basics of Korean cuisine are not difficult to master.

Many people have the mistaken belief that making Korean food is a labor-intensive process. Maybe it's all those photos of women crouched over giant bowls while making kimchi or the large tables of what looks to be hundreds of little dishes laid out for a royal banquet. Sure, there are some meals that may take an army of people to put together, but that's true

of all cuisines. In modern time, Koreans, like everyone else, have to go to work, wrangle their kids, run their errands, and still get dinner on the table.

Korean cuisine emerged from centuries of life on a small peninsula at the edge of the Asian continent. Bordering China to the north and surrounded by oceans on its other three sides, Korea is graced with thousands of miles of coast, mountainous terrain, and fertile plains created by meandering rivers. The people have enjoyed foods from both farming the land and gathering from the sea for generations.

Korean cuisine ranges from bold flavors, infused with the aromas of garlic and chiles, to the more subtle delicacies of royal cuisine, enjoyed by the heirs of its long-lasting dynasties. Regional dishes have emerged over the years—ranging from special fruits or vegetables grown in an area to specific seafoods found near coastal towns.

Contrasts and complements are prevalent in Korean meals. Hot dishes are paired with cool liquids; spicy noodles are eaten with mild vegetables. As in their everyday lives, people strive to create a balance, yin and yang, on their dining table.

Simple white rice serves as the base of most meals (unless you're having noodles or porridge). Koreans eat rice for breakfast, lunch, and dinner, with no distinctions amongst the meals. In fact, the word for meal is synonymous with the word for rice, *bap*. In addition to individual portions of rice, everyone is served a bowl of soup. The accompanying soups are usually uncomplicated affairs, such as Seaweed Soup (page 52) or Bean Sprout Soup (page 55).

Present at every meal is the infamous kimchi. The most popular is the traditional napa cabbage variety (I've provided a simplified version of the recipe on page 107), but it's not uncommon to have two or more varieties available at the same meal. Served in small bowls, kimchi adds an extra kick to whatever else is on the table, even if other dishes may be red with chiles already.

Dining is a communal affair in Korea. All the side dishes *(banchan)* are laid out in the middle of the table for everyone to share. For an everyday meal, there may not be a main dish, but a number of smaller dishes to eat with the rice. The starring attraction might be a bubbling hot pot on a cold night, a lovely plate of barbecued beef for a summer lunch, or a grilled fish seasoned with a bit of sea salt. Whatever

vegetables are in season make their way to the table, as well as some dried fish or pickled seafood.

A Korean meal is generally not served in courses, like a classic Western meal, but all at once. Everyone eats and talks and eats and talks until their rice bowls are empty. Leftover side dishes are usually saved for the next meal. It's a fun way to eat since even picky eaters can choose what they want, while the more adventurous can try a bit of everything.

Even a decade ago, Korean food was considered one of Asia's best-kept secrets. Now the secret is out, and most of us have tried Korean cuisine at neighborhood barbecue joints or have had meals made for us by our Korean friends.

Luckily, ingredients for making delicious Korean meals are readily available. Soy sauce, sesame oil, sesame seeds, and garlic are available at any grocery store. Most Asian markets carry a variety of noodles, dried seaweed, chile powder, and rice flour. Korean groceries can be found in most major metropolitan areas, and the Internet makes it easy to order condiments and goods from even the remotest of areas (I've provided a list of Internet mail-order sources on page 159).

Cooking Korean food at home doesn't require many unusual tools or new equipment. All you need to get started are some large bowls for mixing, a big skillet with a nice flat bottom, and a good sharp knife.

When making a weeknight meal for my family, I first put on a pot of water to boil (since that's the thing that takes the longest). The water will be ready to make noodles or soup. After putting the water on, I prepare the rice. I let my rice cooker do its job while I make the rest of the meal. Even if I forgot to marinate a dish earlier, I can do it right then, letting the meat soak in the flavors while I cook all the other foods. I might stir-fry vegetables with some garlic and sesame oil or just fry up a fish. By the time the button on the rice cooker has popped up, I'm usually done with the meal. And that boiling water, if I didn't need it for noodles or soup, I use to make hot tea.

I hope this book can help you painlessly put a Korean meal on your table. I've included simple but delicious recipes that require a minimal amount of effort without sacrificing flavor.

Your way of cooking may be different than mine, but whatever you do, I hope Korean food makes its way into your repertoire. Feel free to experiment and make these recipes your own. Add more garlic if you want; use less chile paste if you don't like it too spicy. There are no hard and fast rules for cooking. The food police won't come knocking at your door because you substituted a different chile powder for the Korean variety.

The joy of cooking is sharing your efforts with your friends and family. Laugh and talk and eat and laugh until your rice bowls are empty and your bellies are full. Even if it's your first time experimenting, there's no such thing as a bad meal when you're enjoying good company and food made with love.

pantry notes

The Korean pantry can be filled with all kinds of dried plants and goods from the ocean, but you won't need many of them for everyday cooking. Many of the essential ingredients you probably have on hand already, but you can check the glossary (see page 21) if any of them are unfamiliar to you.

I've divided the items into three sections. The A-list includes ingredients used most often and generally found in a Korean kitchen. The B-list consists of items you should keep on hand if you plan to make Korean food often. C-list items are used occasionally and are worth having if you want to delve deeply into expanding your knowledge of the cuisine.

Most of the items can be found in Asian groceries (I have a pretty comprehensive list of them that I keep updated on my Web site, www.eatingkorean.com). I've also provided a list of Internet and mail-order sources (see page 159) in case you want the convenience of having groceries delivered to your door.

These days it's so easy to find the ingredients needed to make Korean food that there's no better time to get started on your culinary journey. So roll up your sleeves, cook up some food, and get eating!

A-LIST INGREDIENTS

Garlic (MANEUL)

Ginger (SAENG-GAHNG)

Short-grain rice (SSAL)

Toasted sesame seeds (GGAE)

Sesame oil (CHANGILEUM)

Soy sauce (GANJANG)

Korean chile paste (GOCHUJANG)

Korean chile powder (GOCHU GALU)

Rice vinegar (CHO)

Various noodles, such as somen,
     sweet potato (JAPCHAE) noodles,
     and buckwheat (NAENGMYEON) noodles

B-LIST INGREDIENTS

Pine nuts (JAT)

Coarse sea salt or kosher salt

Korean malt syrup (MOOL YUT)

Rice flour (SSAL GALU)

Dried anchovies (MYEOLCHI)

Toasted laver/seaweed sheets (GIM)

Korean rice wine (CHONGJU)

Soju

C-LIST INGREDIENTS

White pepper

Black sesame seeds

Rice sticks (DDUKBOKGI DDUK)

Sliced rice cakes (DDEOKGOOK DDUK)

Fish cakes

Kelp/seaweed (MIYEOK)

Thin, wrinkled threads or strands of kelp/seaweed (MIYEOK)

Thicker, flat sheets of kelp/seaweed (DASHIMA)

Fish sauce

Red beans (POT)

Curry sauce (KALEH)

Dried shiitake mushrooms (PYONGO BUHSEOT)

Yellow pickled radish (DANMUJI)

Black bean sauce (JJAJANG)

Sticky/glutinous rice (CHAPSSAL)

Chestnuts (BAHM)

Jujubes/dried red dates (DAECHU)

glossary of korean ingredients

ANCHOVIES (MYEOLCHI) – If you go to the dried goods aisle of your Korean (or other Asian) grocery store, you'll find bags of little fish of varying sizes. The smaller ones are usually sautéed and eaten, while the larger varieties are best for making soup stock.

ASIAN PEAR (NAJU BAE) – These crisp fruits come in season as the air grows colder and the leaves change color. Larger ones are found in Asian groceries, but they can be found often in the produce section of any grocery store. They're best eaten with their brown skins peeled.

ASIAN RADISH OR DAIKON (MU) – Koreans use a variety of radishes in their cooking. The large bulbous varieties can be found in Asian markets, and even in the produce sections of regular groceries, but the smaller ponytail variety *(yulmu)* can only be found in some Asian groceries and farmer's markets. You can store them in the warmer part of the refrigerator for at most a week.

KOREAN CHILE PASTE (GOCHUJANG) – Korean chile paste can be found in jars or plastic tubs in either the condiment aisle or the refrigerated section of Korean markets. Tightly sealed in its original container, it'll keep in the refrigerator almost forever (although you'll lose some spiciness and the bright red color). There really is no substitute for it. If you like spicy food, it's good to keep a small jar around to make hot pots or to spice up your marinades.

CHILE POWDER (GOCHU GALU) – Korean chile powder is different from the regular chile powder you might find in the spice aisle. Sold in large resealable bags, varieties are available in different grades of coarseness and spiciness—usually hot to really hot. The medium-fine powder is the most versatile. It's best to pay extra for high quality, since you'll be using it in many dishes. You can store it in the refrigerator or freezer in a tightly sealed container almost indefinitely.

CHILES (GOCHU) –Although Koreans like chiles of many varieties, the most commonly used ones are the long green variety. Even if they are from the same plant, these chiles can range from totally mild to spicy-hot, depending on what time of the year they are picked (sometimes a chile will be hotter the closer you get to the stem). As they ripen on the vine, they are allowed to turn red and are then dried in the sun to make chile powder *(gochu galu, above)*.

CUCUMBERS (OI) – The smaller pickling cucumbers are used in Korean cooking, but you can substitute the Persian variety as well.

DRIED RED DATES (DAECHU) – See Jujubes.

EGGPLANTS (GAJI) – Korean eggplants are small with smooth dark skins. Japanese varieties, which are very similar, and their paler-skinned Chinese cousins make suitable substitutes. However, the large Italian varieties don't quite work as well in Korean dishes.

FERMENTED SOYBEAN PASTE (DWENJANG) — Korean fermented soybean paste is the color of yellow ochre and chunky in texture. Jars and plastic bins of the paste can be found in the refrigerated section of Korean markets. Although similar to Japanese miso, *dwenjang* is not as sweet, is a bit saltier, and has an earthier flavor.

FISH (MOOL GOGI) — You can find most varieties of fish in the seafood section of Asian groceries. Prepared fish (already cleaned and gutted) are usually available there, too. Fish that are already sliced and ready to be cooked are to be found in the frozen section.

FISH CAKES — Fish cakes are cooked and processed whitefish formed into cakes or loaves (sort of like "krab"). They can be found in the refrigerated section of Asian markets. Koreans usually use the ones that are shaped into flat rectangles and are brown on the outside.

FISH SAUCE — Our family uses this Southeastern Asian condiment to make kimchi, since it's more versatile than salted shrimp or other salted seafood that are traditionally a part of kimchi recipes.

GARLIC (MANEUL) — Although garlic is not native to the peninsula, Koreans eat more garlic than anyone else in the world. Choose firm bulbs that are compact and not sprouting and store in a cool, dark, well-ventilated place. You can find peeled and even minced garlic in Korean markets, in the produce and refrigerated sections respectively. If you're planning on using a lot of garlic, you can mince a bunch and freeze it in small packets tightly wrapped in plastic.

GINGER (SAENG-GANG) — When buying ginger, look for the hardest and heaviest tubers with the smoothest skins. Ginger can be frozen, but you'll lose its crisp texture. Store ginger in the refrigerator for 2 to 3 weeks.

GREEN BEAN SPROUTS (SOOKJU NAMOOL) — See Mung Bean Sprouts.

GREEN ONIONS (PA) — Used to add color and flavor to many Korean recipes, green onions are usually less expensive in Asian, Latino, or Middle Eastern grocery stores than your regular supermarket. Choose firm stalks with dark green tops and thin white ends. They don't last more than a few days but will last longer if you keep them wrapped in damp paper towels in plastic bags in your refrigerator's crisper.

JUJUBES OR DRIED RED DATES (DAECHU) — Found in the dried goods section of Korean groceries, these goodies have wrinkled, brick-red skins with dried brown fruit surrounding a seed inside. They are freshest in late autumn but can be found year round.

KELP/SEAWEED (MIYEOK OR DASHIMA) — Look for this seaweed (sold in long, flat sheets, or thin wrinkled threads or strands) in the dried goods section of Korean and other

Asian markets. The dried plant can be reconstituted by soaking it in water for about 10 minutes. The *miyeok* is softer and used to make soup, while the *dashima* is harder and eaten deep-fried.

KOREAN LEEKS (BUCHU) — Sold in small bundles in the produce section of Korean markets, Korean leeks (sometimes called Korean chives) look like bunches of long grasses but have a mild chive flavor. It's best to buy them the day you're going to eat them and no sooner than the day before. Store them in the refrigerator wrapped in paper towels for just a couple of days.

LAVER/SEAWEED (GIM) — Sold in thin, rectangular sheets, laver can be found in the dried goods section of most Asian groceries. Used to wrap rice rolls, the best ones are already toasted. Korean markets also sell the sheets toasted and seasoned with sesame oil and salt. These sheets are usually served in small squares to be eaten as a wrap for rice.

MALT SYRUP (MOOL YUT) — This thick syrup made from barley, corn, or other grains is used to add some sweetness and shine to meat dishes. It can be found in the condiment aisle of Korean groceries and sometimes in health food stores. You can substitute corn syrup, but use about half the quantity called for since corn syrup is a lot sweeter.

MUNG BEAN SPROUTS (NOKDU NAMOOL) — These sprouts (sometimes labeled "green bean sprouts" or *sookju namool*) can be found next to the soybean sprouts in the produce section of Korean groceries. Mung bean and green bean sprouts can be used interchangeably in Korean cooking. They look very similar but don't have the large yellow head of their soybean cousin.

MUSHROOMS (BUHSEOT) — Many mushroom varieties found in Korea aren't imported, but *pyongo* mushrooms (known here as shiitake) can be used in most Korean recipes and are easily found fresh or dried in Asian groceries. Although fresh mushrooms always taste the best, you can reconstitute the dried mushrooms by soaking them in warm water, stem side down, for about 30 minutes.

NAPA CABBAGE (BAECHU) — Used to make the most popular type of kimchi, napa cabbage can be found in Asian markets and even in some regular grocery stores. Look for tightly packed heads with unblemished leaves and uncracked bodies. (If there are cracks in the white stem ends, it means they have been victims of frost.)

NOODLES (GOOKSU) — Knife noodles *(kal gooksu)* and buckwheat noodles can be found in the refrigerated and frozen sections of Korean markets. Most other noodles, like sweet potato noodles, somen, and buckwheat noodles, can be found in the dried goods section of Korean (and most Asian) groceries.

OCTOPUS (NAKJI) – Look for fresh octopus in the seafood section of most Asian groceries. They should be firm to the touch, grayish white, and have slightly translucent skins. The glossy skin should be peeled before cooking.

PERILLA LEAVES (GGAETNIP) – Originally from southern China, *perilla* (or wild sesame) has leaves that have a strong flavor. Fresh leaves are sold in bundles in the produce section of most Asian markets. Look for dark green leaves with no brown spots. You should buy them the day you plan to use them, since they'll keep in the refrigerator only for a couple of days.

RED BEANS (POT) – Dried red beans can be found in the dried goods section of Asian groceries.

RICE (SSAL OR BAP) – The short-grain rice favored by Koreans can be found in pretty much any grocery store these days, but the Asian stores sell it in large bags. The freshest rice is available in late autumn, after the new harvest hits the stores.

SWEET, GLUTINOUS, OR STICKY RICE (CHAPSSAL) – Used mainly for making desserts, this rice looks like an opaque version of regular short-grain rice. The grains become translucent, chewy, and sticky when cooked. It can be found in the dried goods section of Asian markets.

RICE CAKE OVALETTES (DDUK GOOK DDUK) – These thin rice cakes are made from slicing long cylinders of molded cooked rice. Used to make soup, they are found in the refrigerated or frozen section of Korean groceries. Fresh ones are usually available in the "bakery" section around Lunar New Year.

RICE CAKE STICKS (DDUKBOKGI DDUK) – Usually found in the refrigerated or frozen section of Korean groceries, these little cylinders are sometimes found fresh in the "bakery" section as well.

RICE FLOUR (SSAL GALU) – Found in the dried goods section of Korean (and other Asian) markets, rice flour can be stored just like regular wheat flour.

REFINED RICE WINE (CHONGJU) – Rice wine comes in many forms, but the refined type, *chongju*, is used in cooking, while the distilled *soju* is the most popular for drinking. You can find both in Korean grocery stores.

SALT (SOGEUM) – Coarse sea salt, mostly used to make kimchi, can be found in large bags in Korean markets. It's okay to substitute kosher salt or regular sea salt to use in the recipes.

SESAME OIL (CHANGILEUM) — Koreans like to use the dark sesame oil made from toasted sesame seeds. Look for a rich oil with a strong, nutty aroma, making sure that the oil isn't rancid. Store the oil in the refrigerator to keep it fresher longer.

SESAME SEEDS (GGAE) — Koreans like to use toasted sesame seeds, usually sprinkling them over everything as a garnish. Crushing them between your fingers as you sprinkle brings out more of their nutty flavor. The seeds can be found in most grocery stores. Keep them refrigerated to stay fresh longer.

SOJU — This Korean alcohol was traditionally made from rice, but nowadays manufacturers use less expensive starches (like potatoes, sweet potatoes, and barley). A clear distilled liquid, its alcohol content varies from 20 to 45 percent by volume. It's usually compared to vodka and can be used in place of it in cocktail recipes.

SOYBEAN SPROUTS (KOHNG NAMOOL) — Sometimes labeled simply "bean sprouts," they can be found in the produce section of most Asian groceries. They are thin and white with a large yellow bean head.

SQUID (OJING-UH) — Fresh squid can be found in the seafood section of most Asian markets, but Korean markets also sell them cleaned and sliced in the freezer section. Dried squid strips are available in the dried goods section of most Asian markets as well.

SWEET POTATOES OR YAMS (GOGUMA) — Korean yams come into season in the late fall. Although regular sweet potatoes can be substituted, Korean varieties are smaller and sweeter and can be found in the produce section of most Asian markets.

WAKAME (MIYEOK) — Found in the dried good section of many Asian groceries, these thin strands of seaweed are used mainly in soups.

ZUCCHINI OR SQUASH (HOBAK) — There are a variety of different squashes used in Korean cuisine. Korean summer squashes resemble Italian zucchini, which can be easily substituted for them.

useful utensils for cooking korean food

GIANT BOWLS AND TINY SAUCERS

You'll want to have some bowls large enough for serving one-dish meals, like most of the recipes in the Noodles chapter. Smaller bowls are useful for all the little side dishes and for individual servings of rice and soup. Tiny saucers will come in handy for Pickled Garlic (page 113) or Pickled Peppers (page 112) and for sides of various sauces (pages 155).

You'll also need a couple of pretty large mixing bowls if you plan on making kimchi or marinating meat. They're also useful to hold the batter for your flat cakes.

Good bowls and sauce dishes are available in any Asian houseware store or even in Asian groceries, although your selection will be much more limited. If you have young children (or a clumsy spouse), they're also available in Chinese fast-food plastic. On the other end of the spectrum, you can purchase handmade artisan wares in specialized pottery shops as well.

GOOD KNIVES AND CUTTING BOARDS

As with most cuisines in which chopsticks are the main eating utensil, Korean food is usually cut into bite-size pieces to make it easier to eat. Good knives are not only essential in Korean cooking but also are useful for all your culinary endeavors. The least you can get by with is a good 10-inch chef's knife. The broad side is great for smashing garlic (smash the clove whole and the peel comes right off), and a good sharp edge makes cutting everything a cinch. A paring knife will also come in handy for trimming vegetables.

As for cutting boards, try to have at least two around—one for cutting meats and fish and the other for vegetables and fruits. This helps avoid contamination between raw meats and other foods.

SKILLETS AND FRYING PANS

One of the most versatile things you can get before embarking on your Korean food odyssey is a large skillet with a good lid (I prefer glass lids so I can see the food inside). You'll need a flat nonstick surface for making flat cakes. If you plan on making flat cakes often or would like to cook your meat on the table (like they do in the restaurants), an electric frying pan is a nice thing to have. Although not as fun as a grill built into your tabletop, it works just as well and keeps you from having to leave the table to cook the food.

POTS

You'll want to have a large pot for cooking noodles or making big batches of soup. Medium pots with heavy bottoms and lids are good for hot pots and for deep-frying. If you want to be extra fancy, you can get a stone pot, which is not only good for making hot pots but also for serving Mixed Rice Bowl (page 119), but in that case you'll need more than one.

SPATULAS, LONG CHOPSTICKS, WOODEN SPOONS, AND LADLES

A good flat-bottom spatula is great for flipping flat cakes. A pair of long, wooden chopsticks will serve you well not only for stir-frying but also for deep-frying. You can use a regular wooden spoon for sautéing as well. If you're making a noodle soup, you'll want to use a combination of a ladle and the long chopsticks to serve the food. Long chopsticks are inexpensive and easy to find. You may like them so much that you use them for more than Asian cooking.

RICE COOKER

An electric rice cooker is an indispensable appliance in a Korean kitchen. Simply wash the rice, measure, and add the water, then push a button. The rice will cook all by itself, leaving you free to make the rest of the meal. I've found that the rice cookers with tops that seal and lock shut are better than the ones with glass lids that just rest on top. Those tend to splatter a bit when cooking, although the rice will cook well just the same. I suggest splurging on a larger rice cooker (even if you're cooking for just one), since you may want to make more servings occasionally. Besides, it doesn't hurt to have leftover rice for fried rice the next day.

LARGE GLASS JARS

If you plan on making kimchi or doing some pickling, you'll want a large glass jar. For large batches, opt for a 5-gallon one. If you're only making enough for one or two people, a 1-gallon jar will suffice.

FOOD PROCESSOR

A food processor is great for chopping onions, mincing garlic, and any number of activities needed to make marinades and sauces in Korean cooking. Some Asian kitchenware stores also sell mini food processors, which are convenient for mincing garlic and ginger for kimchi and other things. It is definitely not a necessity but nice to have if you prefer the gadgets to do the work for you.

appetizers and snacks

THE DISHES IN THIS CHAPTER CAN BE EATEN WITH YOUR FINGERS, shared with your friends at a party, or made for your kids when they get home from school. I grew up eating all of this food, and each recipe is filled with memories. The Rice Cake Stick Snack (page 33) was an after-school favorite of mine and is still a favorite street food throughout the alleyways of Seoul. Any one of the pancakes in this chapter makes a great snack, appetizer, or light lunch. I've also included one porridge *(jook)* dish, the Black Sesame Porridge (page 39). A comfortable and healthful food, porridge comes in both sweet and savory varieties. I could write a whole chapter on porridges, but there just wasn't enough room in this book for it. The porridge makes a lovely breakfast on a cold morning or a stick-to-your-ribs afternoon snack.

The rest of the batter-based dishes in the chapter are traditional Korean *janchi* (party) food, since you can whip up a big batch and fry enough for you and dozens of your guests. Instead of the usual large quantities made for parties, I've whittled the recipes down to a manageable size. Of course, feel free to double or quadruple the amounts for your next weekend fiesta. Or make some for you and that special someone. You can have your very own party any night of the week.

rice cake stick snack
(ddukbokgi)

Ddukbokgi is one of the many wonderful street foods you can buy as an after-school snack or to have with your beer after work. If you don't like it spicy, leave out the chile paste and add a little more soy sauce and sugar to suit your taste. If using refrigerated or frozen rice sticks, separate them and soak them in cold water to soften for at least an hour, but fresh rice cake sticks are, of course, the best. The malt syrup, fish cakes, and rice cake sticks can be found at any Korean grocery store.

In a large skillet, heat the vegetable oil over medium-high heat. Add the onion and carrot and stir-fry for a couple of minutes, until the carrot becomes a bit soft.

Add the rice cake sticks (make sure they are separated first), chile paste, soy sauce, sesame oil, sugar (or malt syrup), and fish cakes. Continue stir-frying for another 5 minutes or so. If the rice cake sticks are still hard, lower the heat a bit, cover, and let steam for a couple of minutes to soften.

Increase the heat (if you've lowered it), add the green onions, and cook for another 2 to 3 minutes. Sprinkle with toasted sesame seeds, if you wish, and serve immediately.

VARIATION:
Koreans put everything from vegetables to ramen noodles in this dish. Instead of fish cakes, you can add boolgogi *(page 83) or any type of mushroom, which you would cook with the onion and carrot.*

**MAKES 5 OR 6 SERVINGS
AS A SNACK**

1 tablespoon vegetable oil
1 onion, sliced
1 carrot, thinly sliced
2 pounds rice cake sticks *(ddukbokgi dduk)*
1 tablespoon Korean chile paste
1 tablespoon soy sauce
1 tablespoon Asian sesame oil
1 tablespoon sugar or Korean
    malt syrup *(mool yut)*
2 fish cakes, cut into strips
2 green onions, cut into 1-inch pieces
Toasted sesame seeds for garnish

pan-fried beef in egg batter

(gogi jeon)

Traditionally enjoyed during a celebration, this dish makes an excellent appetizer or side dish. Get the *boolgogi* (sliced rib-eye) cut of meat at your Korean grocery, or ask your butcher to slice a lean cut as thinly as he can. When cooking the beef, I like to use wooden chopsticks to dip and fry the meat, but a spatula works just as well for flipping.

- Cut the beef into 2- to 3-inch pieces. Lightly salt and pepper the beef on both sides.

- Pour enough flour onto a plate to cover the plate. Then flour the meat on both sides, leaving the pieces stacked in the flour.

- In a small bowl, whisk the egg until lightly beaten. Set aside.

- Preheat a large, nonstick pan over medium-low heat, adding just enough oil to thinly cover the pan. Dip the floured beef into the egg, making sure it is well-coated on both sides and carefully place onto the hot pan. Repeat until all the beef pieces are in the pan. Let cook on both sides until the meat is browned completely, but the egg is not too browned. Add more oil as needed.

- Serve warm with a side of Seasoned Soy Sauce (page 155).

MAKES 3 TO 4 APPETIZER SERVINGS

½ pound beef, sliced thinly
Freshly ground black pepper
Salt
All-purpose flour for dusting
1 large egg
Vegetable oil for frying

green onion pancakes

(pa jeon)

This vegetarian dish can be eaten as a snack, appetizer, or light meal. Rice flour gives the flat cakes a slightly chewier, stickier texture. If you can't find that, feel free to add more all-purpose flour instead, although your pancakes won't be as chewy. If there are any left, refrigerate or freeze them but reheat in a skillet (not the microwave) to keep the edges nice and crispy.

✿ Combine the flour, rice flour, salt, and black pepper, if using. Add about 2 cups cold water and stir. Stir in more water if needed, a little at a time, until the mixture is the consistency of thin pancake batter.

✿ Add the green onions, zucchini, and carrot to the batter and mix.

✿ In a large skillet or on a griddle, add just enough vegetable oil to thinly cover the surface. Turn the heat to medium-high. After the oil is heated, spoon enough batter into the skillet to make a large flat circle 6 to 8 inches in diameter.

✿ Cook on one side until golden brown, then flip the pancake and cook the other side. Reduce the heat as necessary to prevent burning. Remove the pancake. Repeat with the remaining batter, adding more oil as needed. Serve them fresh off the griddle with Seasoned Soy Sauce.

VARIATION:
For a little color and different flavors, add julienned red bell pepper, mushrooms, onion, and/or Korean leeks (found in Korean groceries, they look like bunches of long grass but have a mild leek flavor). You can even add ham, shrimp, or leftover turkey to the batter, too.

MAKES 6 TO 8 FLAT CAKES,
SERVING 4 TO 6 AS AN APPETIZER

1½ cups all-purpose flour
½ cup rice flour
1 teaspoon salt
Dash of freshly ground black pepper (optional)
2 cups cold water, plus more as needed
6 green onions, cut into 1½-inch lengths
2 Korean or Italian zucchini,
    coarsely grated or julienned
1 carrot, coarsely grated or julienned
Vegetable oil for frying
Seasoned Soy Sauce (page 155)

⅓ recipe.

korean leek pancakes
(buchu buchingae)

Korean leeks look like a bundle of long grasses but have a bit of a chive flavor. You can find them in the produce section of Korean groceries. I've provided a vegetarian version of this pancake for you, but feel free to add bits of shrimp or other types of meat if you wish. Instead of red bell pepper, you can add a red jalapeño if you want it to have some kick. Although these flat cakes are traditionally made for special feasts, they make a nice snack or appetizer any day of the week.

- Combine the flour, rice flour, egg, and water in a mixing bowl. The consistency should be that of thin pancake batter.

- Add the leeks, red pepper, salt, and pepper and combine.

- Heat about 1 tablespoon oil in a large skillet over medium-high heat. With a ladle, spoon about a cup of the batter into the pan and spread it thin and wide into a large circle about 8 inches in diameter. Cook until the edges get slightly brown and the center starts becoming slightly translucent, 3 to 4 minutes. Flip the pancake and cook on the other side for 3 to 4 minutes. Place the cooked pancake on a cutting board.

- Repeat until all of the batter is used, stacking the pancakes on top of each other. Carefully cut the pancakes into wedges or other manageable pieces and serve immediately with Seasoned Soy Sauce for dipping.

MAKES 5 TO 10 APPETIZER SERVINGS

1½ cups all-purpose flour
½ cup rice flour
1 large egg
2 cups cold water, plus more as needed
2 bundles Korean leeks, cut into 2-inch lengths
½ red bell pepper, julienned
1 teaspoon salt
¼ teaspoon freshly ground white pepper
Vegetable oil for frying
Seasoned Soy Sauce (page 155)

kimchi pancakes

(gimchi buchingae)

This is a great dish to make when your leftover *baechu* (napa cabbage) kimchi is past its prime. In fact, the riper your kimchi, the tastier the pancakes will be. You can use any other meat (beef, chicken, shrimp, squid/calamari), but pork seems to taste best. It's faster to make your pancakes large and then cut them for serving. However, if you wish, you can make them into smaller (about 6-inch) rounds.

🍳 In a large bowl, combine the flour, rice flour, water, and egg and mix lightly. The mixture should be the consistency of pancake batter but doesn't have to be smooth. Add a little more water if necessary but remember that the kimchi will add liquid as well. Stir in the kimchi, green onions, pork, and salt.

🍳 In a large skillet, heat about 1 tablespoon oil over medium-high heat. Ladle batter into the skillet and spread it out to an 8-inch circle. Cook until the edges turn brown and crispy, 3 to 4 minutes. Flip it over, add a little bit more oil around the pancake, and cook for another 3 minutes or so until cooked through. Repeat with the remaining batter, adding oil as needed. Serve the pancakes hot out of the skillet. Cut into wedges or serve whole.

MAKES ABOUT 4 LARGE PANCAKES,
SERVING 4 TO 6 AS AN APPETIZER

1 cup all-purpose flour

½ cup rice flour

1½ cups cold water, plus more as needed

1 large egg

1 cup *baechu* kimchi, coarsely chopped
(page 107)

2 green onions, cut into 1-inch pieces

3 ounces uncooked pork, chopped

½ teaspoon salt

Vegetable oil for frying

black sesame porridge

(ggae jook)

Rice porridges *(jook)* are a popular part of Korean cuisine. Eaten as a light breakfast, a warm snack, or what Koreans call "well-being" food, porridge comes in both sweet and savory varieties. The basic way of making porridge is explained here. Feel free to try variations of your own. You can make sweet versions with red beans or pumpkin, and savory porridges with abalone, clams, or whatever you like. This elegant porridge makes a lovely appetizer for a dinner party or a hearty breakfast.

Soak the rice in water to cover for at least 2 hours or overnight. Drain.

In a blender or food processor, grind the rice with 1 cup of the water, adding more water a tablespoon at a time if needed. Add the sesame seeds and process until the mixture becomes a chunky paste, adding more water if needed.

Put the black rice mixture in a medium pan and stir in about 3 cups water. Let simmer over medium heat for about 20 minutes, stirring occasionally and breaking up any lumps as needed. Reduce the heat and let simmer an additional 10 to 15 minutes, stirring more frequently as the porridge thickens. It should be the consistency of oatmeal.

Divide the porridge among 4 individual bowls and sprinkle with pine nuts. Serve warm with sugar or honey and salt on the side.

NOTE:
If the porridge seems to be taking a long time to thicken, add a teaspoon or two of rice flour to thicken.

MAKES 4 SERVINGS

1 cup short-grain rice
About 4 cups water, plus more as needed
½ cup black sesame seeds
Toasted pine nuts for garnish
Sugar or honey for serving
Salt for serving

deep-fried squid

(ojing-uh twigim)

This is the Korean version of fried calamari, but the squid is cooked in strips rather than rings. Another popular street food, it makes a good snack, appetizer, or finger food. Double or triple the recipe for a big party.

🌀 Prepare the squid by peeling off the skin and cutting into ¼-inch-wide strips.

🌀 Combine the flour, salt, pepper, baking powder, and ½ cup water in a medium bowl. Add more water if necessary, 1 tablespoon at a time, until the mixture is the consistency of thick pancake batter.

🌀 In a deep heavy pan, heat about 1 inch oil to 375° F. Depending on the size of your pan, dust about half the squid pieces with flour, dip in the batter, then carefully place in the preheated oil. (I like to use long wooden chopsticks for this part, but you can use tongs or any other tool that works for you.) Let cook until golden. Repeat with the remaining squid.

🌀 Serve immediately with Vinegar Soy Sauce for dipping.

MAKES 3 OR 4 APPETIZER SERVINGS

8 ounces cleaned squid
1 cup all-purpose flour, plus more for dusting
1 teaspoon salt
1 teaspoon freshly ground black pepper
½ teaspoon baking powder
½ cup cold water, plus more as needed
Vegetable oil for deep-frying
Vinegar Soy Sauce (page 155)

fried oysters

(gool jeon)

I love oysters raw, cooked, barbecued—pretty much every which way. Fried in this traditional egg batter, they make a flavorful start to any dinner party, a nice afternoon snack, or a good *anju* (drinking snack) to go with an ice-cold beer. For this recipe, I like to use frozen oysters available in most Asian markets, since they are already shucked and ready to go.

↯ Drain the oysters and sprinkle with the ginger, black pepper, and salt. Let sit.

↯ Whisk the eggs in a medium bowl.

↯ Heat 2 to 3 tablespoons vegetable oil in a large skillet over medium heat.

↯ Pour some flour onto a plate and dust the oysters. Dip the dusted oysters one at a time in the egg and carefully place in the hot skillet. Cook until they are golden brown on both sides, about 3 minutes on each side, adding more oil and adjusting the heat as needed.

↯ Serve immediately with Seasoned Soy Sauce for dipping.

MAKES 8 TO 12 APPETIZER SERVINGS

1 pound shucked oysters
1 tablespoon grated fresh ginger
¼ teaspoon freshly ground black pepper
⅛ teaspoon salt
3 large eggs
Vegetable oil for frying
All-purpose flour for dusting
Seasoned Soy Sauce (page 155)

soups and hot pots

INDIVIDUAL BOWLS OF SOUP OR A STONE POT BUBBLING WITH A SPICY stew are present at almost every meal in Korea. Instead of water or a beverage, the soup serves as the liquid to help wash everything down. The Bean Sprout Soup (page 55) and Seaweed Soup (page 52) are healthful as well as delicious. And both of the Dough Flake Soups (pages 47 and 48) and the Dumpling Soup with Rice Cakes (page 51) are hearty enough to serve as a meal in themselves.

Hot pots, such as the kimchi version (page 53), are usually shared by the whole table. Although Koreans dip their spoons right into the pot, you may want to provide small bowls and a ladle so people can spoon out what they want for themselves.

You'd think that these steaming dishes would be great only for cold weather meals, but Koreans eat soup all year round. So get your spoons ready to enjoy a good warm dish any time of year.

dough flake soup with potatoes

(gamja sujebi)

Gamja sujebi is popular in the most mountainous areas of Korea, such as the province of Gangwon-do. The rocky terrain makes it hard to grow rice and other flatland loving grains, but potatoes can be grown along the hillsides. A Korean comfort food, this soup is a great meal for when the weather is just turning chilly and the leaves are taking on their brilliant fall colors.

Combine the flour and ¼ cup of the water. Stir in the remaining water a bit at a time until the dough clumps together. Knead and form into a ball. Wrap tightly in plastic (or place in a sealed plastic bag) and refrigerate for about 1 hour (or overnight).

In the meantime, prepare the Anchovy Stock and cut the vegetables. If it's not simmering already, bring the stock to a boil, add the garlic and potato, and let cook for about 3 minutes. Add the zucchini and cook for another 2 to 3 minutes.

Remove the dough from the refrigerator. Rip the dough into flat, bite-size pieces about an inch or so large (they can be rough with uneven edges) and add them to the boiling stock as you do so. Don't worry about the shape being irregular—the rough shape is part of the charm. Keep adding until you've used up all the dough. Let cook until the dough pieces begin to float and become slightly translucent around the edges, 5 to 7 minutes (thicker pieces will take a bit longer).

Add the green onion and egg without stirring. Add ¼ teaspoon salt and taste (take care not to burn yourself). Add a bit more salt if you like but remember that you'll be eating this with a soy sauce seasoning.

Serve nice and hot with Seasoned Soy Sauce.

MAKES 3 OR 4 SERVINGS

2 cups all-purpose flour
½ cup water
Anchovy Stock (page 157)
2 cloves garlic, minced
1 medium russet or red potato, peeled and cut into ½-inch pieces
1 zucchini, quartered or halved and cut into ½-inch-thick pieces
1 green onion, cut into 2-inch lengths
1 large egg, beaten
¼ teaspoon salt, plus more to taste
Seasoned Soy Sauce (page 155)

NOTE:
If you don't want to bother with the Anchovy Stock, you can use anchovy cubes or powder, which can be found in most Asian markets.

kimchi dough flake soup

(kimchi sujebi)

Easy to make, this soup is great when it's raining outside and you want a hot bowl of soup while listening to the raindrops hit your windowpanes. A basic recipe with no fancy additions, it makes a satisfying lunch or light dinner.

- Combine the flour and ¼ cup of the water. Stir in the remaining water a bit at a time until the dough clumps together. Knead and form into a ball. Wrap tightly in plastic (or place in a sealed plastic bag) and refrigerate for about 1 hour (or overnight).

- In the meantime, prepare the Anchovy Stock and chop the kimchi. If it's not simmering already, bring the stock to a boil. Add the kimchi, its liquid, garlic, and chile paste and bring to a boil again.

- Remove the dough from the refrigerator. Rip the dough into flat, bite-size pieces about an inch or so large and add them to the boiling stock as you do so. Don't worry about the shape and the edges being irregular—the rough shape is part of the charm. Keep adding until you've used up all the dough. Let cook until the dough pieces begin to float and become slightly translucent around the edges, 5 to 7 minutes (thicker pieces will take a bit longer). Add the green onion and salt and let cook for about another minute.

- Carefully taste the soup and add a bit more salt if necessary. Serve immediately.

MAKES 2 OR 3 SERVINGS

2 cups all-purpose flour
½ cup water
Anchovy Stock (page 157)
½ cup kimchi, coarsely chopped,
    with its liquid
2 cloves garlic, minced
1 teaspoon Korean chile paste
1 green onion, cut into 2-inch lengths
¼ teaspoon salt, plus more to taste

tofu hot pot
(soon dubu)

Soon Dubu is one of the only Korean hot pots that is usually served in individual bowls instead of being shared by the whole table. It can be made with shrimp, squid, clams, chicken, pork, other meats, kimchi, or any combination of the above. I've included an easy beef version below. Serve it with a side of rice and some kimchi. The super-soft tofu can be found in the refrigerated section of most Asian markets.

⟐ Combine the chile paste, garlic, salt, and sesame oil in a small bowl.

⟐ Bring the beef and beef stock to a boil in a large pot. Add the chile paste mixture and stir until thoroughly dissolved. Add the tofu and simmer for about 5 minutes. Add the green onions and cook for another minute or two.

⟐ Ladle the soup into individual bowls and immediately add 1 raw egg to each bowl. Serve bubbling hot.

VARIATION:
Soon Dubu *can also be made with kimchi instead of beef, or make a seafood version with tiny shrimp, oysters, clams, and squid.*

MAKES 2 OR 3 SERVINGS

2 tablespoons Korean chile paste *(gochujang)*
2 cloves garlic, minced
2 teaspoons salt
2 teaspoons Asian sesame oil
4 ounces rib-eye or other tender cut of beef,
    thinly sliced into bite-size pieces
2 cups beef stock
9 ounces extra-soft tofu
2 green onions, cut into 1-inch pieces
2 or 3 large eggs

dumpling soup with rice cakes

(ddeok mandu gook)

———•

Dumplings of many varieties and sliced rice cakes can be found in the frozen section of Korean markets. Although you can use any sort of dumpling for this dish, I prefer the traditional pork variety. I have found that kimchi dumplings taste the best when fried, so I am not recommending them for this dish. A popular dish to serve for Lunar New Year *(Sollal)*, this soup will warm you up on any cold day. If you don't have white pepper on hand, just use black pepper.

Bring the Anchovy Stock to a boil in a large pot. Add the dumplings and rice cakes and cook until the rice cakes are soft and the dumplings are cooked through, 5 to 7 minutes. Slowly pour the egg over the boiling liquid, then add the green onions, white pepper, and salt. Let cook for another minute or two and remove from the heat. Taste the broth and add a bit more salt if needed.

Ladle into large bowls, dividing the dumplings equally. Top with a bit of the crumbled seaweed if desired.

MAKES 3 OR 4 SERVINGS

Anchovy Stock (page 157) or
  2½ quarts beef broth
16 dumplings
8 ounces sliced rice cakes
1 large egg, beaten
2 green onions, cut into 2-inch lengths
½ teaspoon freshly ground white pepper
½ teaspoon salt, plus more to taste
1 toasted laver/seaweed sheet,
  crumbled (optional)

seaweed soup

(miyeok gook)

This healthful soup is served to women after they've given birth. It is also prepared for a person's birthday to make him or her another year stronger and healthier. Birthdays or not, I like to make this soup when the wind is strong and there's a chill in the air. This version is based on beef, but you can substitute small oysters, little clams, mussels, or other shellfish if you want to keep it pure with the flavors of the sea.

🥄 Soak the seaweed in water for about 5 minutes. The seaweed will swell up and turn a dark green. Using kitchen shears, cut the seaweed into pieces 2 to 3 inches long.

🥄 Heat a heavy-bottomed medium pot over medium-high heat. Add the beef, garlic, sesame oil, and black pepper to taste and stir-fry until the beef is browned, 2 to 3 minutes. Add the water, soy sauce, and seaweed and bring to a boil. Reduce the heat and simmer for 10 to 15 minutes.

🥄 Taste the soup and add salt if necessary. Serve the soup steaming hot with rice and kimchi.

MAKES 2 OR 3 SERVINGS

1 ounce dried kelp/seaweed *(miyeok)*
4 ounces beef brisket or shank, sliced
1 clove garlic, minced
1 tablespoon Asian sesame oil
Freshly ground black pepper
About 4 cups water
1 tablespoon soy sauce
Salt or soy sauce to taste

kimchi hot pot

(gimchi jjigae)

For some reason, pork and kimchi taste really good together. This recipe is a perfect example of how the meat works well with the spicy flavors of the kimchi. Any sort of pork will do. Boneless cuts are easier to eat, but the bone adds a bit more flavor to the broth. This is a quick main dish that is great for when you have a lot of leftover kimchi around.

⑤ Heat a medium saucepan or stone pot over medium-high heat. Add the pork, sesame oil, chile paste, and garlic and stir-fry until the pork is browned, 4 to 5 minutes.

⑤ Add the kimchi with its liquid and the water and bring to a boil. Reduce the heat and simmer until the pork is cooked through, 6 to 8 minutes, depending on how large your pork pieces are.

⑤ Add the tofu and green onions to the simmering liquid. Simmer until the tofu is heated through, about 2 minutes more.

⑤ Place the hot pot in the middle of the table to be shared with other side dishes.

MAKES ABOUT 4 SERVINGS

4 ounces pork, cut into chunks
1 tablespoon Asian sesame oil
1 tablespoon Korean chile paste
3 cloves garlic, sliced
1 cup napa cabbage *(baechu)* kimchi, (page 107) sliced 1½ inches thick, with its liquid
2 cups water
6 ounces medium-soft tofu, sliced
2 green onions, cut into 2-inch lengths

bean sprout soup

(kohng namool gook)

—●

This simple and nutritious soup made from soybean sprouts is a nice accompaniment to any meal. It's a little spicy but has a tasty broth. Koreans eat this soup as a comfort food, especially when they're down with a cold or flu. Although they're cooked, the sprouts retain their crisp texture. Traditionally, the root ends are trimmed from the sprouts, but leaving them on saves time and doesn't affect the flavor one bit.

- Rinse and drain the sprouts, removing any bean skins.

- Bring the Anchovy Stock to a boil in a large pot, if it's not hot already. Add the sprouts, garlic, chile powder, and sesame oil and bring to a boil. Reduce the heat and simmer for about 10 minutes. Add the salt and green onions and let cook for about a minute more. Carefully taste the soup and add more salt if you think it needs it.

- Serve in individual bowls on the side with any rice dish.

MAKES 5 OR 6 SERVINGS

8 ounces soybean sprouts
Anchovy Stock (page 157)
1 clove garlic, minced
1 teaspoon Korean chile powder
1 teaspoon Asian sesame oil
1 teaspoon salt, plus more to taste
2 green onions, chopped

small side dishes

IF YOU'VE EVER EATEN AT A KOREAN RESTAURANT, YOU'VE SEEN the variety of small *banchan* (side dishes) that come out with your meal. It's customary to have seasonal and regional vegetables on your table. Everyone gets his/her own bowl of rice and a small bowl of soup. The rest of the *banchan* are meant to be shared. They can vary from a variety of kimchi to *namool* (vegetables) with sometimes a star attraction (like a meat or fish dish) or a steaming hot pot.

Because of centuries-old superstition, Koreans set out dishes in odd numbers. So it's better to have five or seven small *banchan* than four or six. For royal meals, it wasn't unusual to have twenty-one different small dishes laid out on the table. Unless you're serving royalty, there's no need to go overboard. Each dish is served in small portions and meant to be finished at each meal. You can always replenish more of the popular items and refrigerate the rest for the next lunch or dinner.

The *banchan* I've collected for this section are some of the most popular ones that can be eaten throughout the year. You can prepare most vegetables by sautéing in a bit of garlic, sesame oil, salt, and sesame seeds. Buddhist monks make a whole meal out of only rice and *sanchae* (wild mountain vegetables) that they've gathered in the mountains near their temples. Although I wouldn't encourage you to go foraging for mushrooms or other things (unless you know what you're doing), you can use the basic recipes to cook up any strange and wonderful greens or vegetables you pick up from your Asian grocer.

seasoned tofu

(dubu jolim)

—

Tofu is one of the best inventions of all time. Not only is it good for you, but it also takes on seasonings really well and comes in a range of textures. I like to use firm tofu for this dish so that it doesn't fall apart when cooking, but in a pinch the medium-firm kind will do as well. This easy side dish is a great addition to any weeknight meal, but it's also good enough to serve at a dinner party.

- Remove the tofu from its package and let it drain in a colander or on its side in a bowl.

- Combine the green onions and garlic in a small bowl. Add the soy sauce, sesame oil, sesame seeds, and chile powder and mix.

- Cut the tofu cube lengthwise in half, then cut into ½-inch-thick slices.

- Heat the vegetable oil in a large skillet over high heat. Carefully place the tofu slices in the skillet. Cook until the tofu is slightly browned on the bottom and getting a bit crispy on the edges, 4 to 5 minutes. Turn the slices over and brown the other side.

- Reduce the heat and spoon the seasoning over the tofu, distributing it somewhat evenly. Cover and let steam for 2 to 3 minutes. Transfer to a plate and serve immediately.

VARIATION:
If you like your food to have a bit of a kick, finely chop ½ jalapeño (remove the seeds, of course) and add it to the soy mixture.

MAKES ABOUT 4 SERVINGS

One 18-ounce package firm tofu
2 green onions, chopped
2 cloves garlic, minced
2 tablespoons soy sauce
1 tablespoon Asian sesame oil
1 tablespoon toasted sesame seeds
1 teaspoon Korean chile powder
1 tablespoon vegetable oil

sautéed potatoes and carrots

(gamja bokkeum)

Whenever my husband complains that there's nothing to eat in the house, this is one of the side dishes I whip up. Since most of us have potatoes, carrots, and onions at home, it's an easy dish to add to a last-minute Korean meal. This particular *banchan* is not fancy, or royal, cuisine, but it is popular with even the pickiest of kids. Although potatoes are a New World crop, Koreans have embraced them. But then again, garlic and chiles aren't native to Korea either, and we wouldn't be able to imagine certain dishes without them.

Heat the vegetable oil in a large skillet over medium heat. Add the potatoes, carrots, and onion. Cover and cook, stirring occasionally, until the potatoes soften and the onion is slightly browned, about 10 minutes.

Add the green onion, salt, and sesame oil and toss. Cook for another minute or so. Sprinkle with sesame seeds and serve immediately.

MAKES 5 TO 7 SERVINGS

1 tablespoon vegetable oil
2 medium potatoes, peeled and cut
   into strips, about ¼- to ½-inch-thin
2 medium carrots, peeled and cut
   into into strips, about ¼- to ½-inch-thin
1 small onion, sliced
1 green onion, chopped
½ teaspoon salt
2 teaspoons Asian sesame oil
1 teaspoon toasted sesame seeds

seasoned spinach

(shigeumchi namool)

When I was a kid, this was one of my favorite dishes to make. Not only was it tasty, but I also loved how the big bunches of spinach would shrink down to just tasty bites. Even now I'll serve this as part of an everyday meal or elaborate feast. Popeye would be proud!

🌀 Bring about ¼ inch water to a boil in a large pot. Add the spinach, cover, and steam until the leaves are just wilted, about 2 minutes. Immediately transfer to a colander and rinse with cold water. Squeeze the water from the spinach and shape it into a ball. Cut the ball in half, then in half again.

🌀 Mix the spinach with the sesame oil, garlic, green onion, sesame seeds, and salt in a medium bowl. Let sit for at least 10 minutes to let the flavors soak in.

🌀 Serve at room temperature or chilled, sprinkled with sesame seeds.

MAKES 4 SERVINGS

2 bunches spinach (about 8 ounces),
  rinsed and trimmed
1 tablespoon Asian sesame oil
2 cloves garlic, minced
1 green onion, chopped
1 teaspoon toasted sesame seeds,
  plus more for garnish
1 teaspoon salt or to taste

sautéed eggplant

(gaji namool)

—

Outdoor markets in Seoul are filled with beautiful purple eggplants when they are in season in late summer. Much smaller than the European varieties, Korean eggplants are similar to their Japanese cousins. The traditional way to make this *banchan* (side dish) is to boil the eggplants first and then shred or cut them, but I've found a method that is much simpler. If you don't like spicy food, you may omit the chile powder, but compared to some other Korean dishes, the heat is barely noticeable.

MAKES 5 OR 6 SERVINGS

1 tablespoon vegetable oil

1 clove garlic, minced

2 medium eggplants, cut into
   ½-inch-thick strips, 2 to 3 inches long

1 tablespoon Asian sesame oil

1 green onion, chopped

1 tablespoon soy sauce

1 teaspoon Korean chile powder

1 teaspoon toasted sesame seeds, crushed

ⓢ Heat the vegetable oil in a large skillet over medium-high heat. Add the garlic and eggplants and stir-fry until the eggplants are limp and starting to brown, 6 to 8 minutes. Add the sesame oil, green onion, soy sauce, and chile powder and stir-fry for another minute or so. Remove from the heat.

ⓢ Sprinkle with sesame seeds and serve either warm or at room temperature.

seasoned zucchini

(hobak namool)

Every spring my mom would plant a handful of *hobak* seeds in our garden. The broad leaves and curling vines would take over the yard, yielding yellow blossoms that eventually grew into firm green squashes. I would love to run barefoot into the backyard to hunt under the leaves for the light green vegetables that would become a tasty part of our dinner. Korean zucchini are fatter, shorter, and lighter skinned than their Italian cousins, but any variety will do. Although I'm too lazy to plant my own *hobak*, I still like to make this easy *banchan* for everyday meals.

Heat the vegetable oil and sesame oil in a large skillet over medium-high heat. Add the zucchini, onion, and garlic and stir-fry until the zucchini starts to brown, 5 to 6 minutes. Add the green onion and salt and cook for another couple of minutes or so. Remove from the heat and let sit for about 10 minutes to let the flavors infuse. Taste and add a little more salt if necessary.

Serve either warm or at room temperature, sprinkled with sesame seeds.

MAKES 5 TO 7 SERVINGS

1 tablespoon vegetable oil

1 tablespoon Asian sesame oil

2 medium zucchini, thinly sliced either in rounds or semicircles

1 small onion, sliced

1 clove garlic, minced

1 green onion, chopped

¼ teaspoon salt or more to taste

1 teaspoon toasted sesame seeds

seasoned mung bean sprouts

(sookju namool)

This is a tasty and easy way to eat any sort of sprout. Although soy sauce is sometimes used to season any number of vegetables *(namool)*, I prefer to use salt to preserve the subtle color of the sprouts. These sprouts (sometimes labeled "green bean sprouts") can be found in the produce section of most Asian markets.

§ Bring the water to a boil in a large pot. In the meantime, rinse the sprouts and discard any bad ones. Place the sprouts in the pot, cover, and blanch for 2 to 3 minutes. Immediately transfer to a colander and rinse with cold water. Drain and squeeze out any excess water.

§ Place the sprouts in a medium bowl. Add the green onions, garlic, sesame seeds, sesame oil, and salt and combine. Serve warm or chilled. Store leftovers in a tightly sealed container in the refrigerator for up to 2 days.

MAKES 8 TO 10 SERVINGS

1 cup water
1 pound mung bean sprouts
2 green onions, chopped
1 clove garlic, minced
1 tablespoon toasted sesame seeds
1 tablespoon Asian sesame oil
1½ teaspoons salt

deep-fried kelp

(dashima twigim)

———

Large sheets of this seaweed can be found in the dry goods aisle of Korean and Japanese (and some Chinese) markets. An easy dish to make, the kelp has several health benefits (although all those benefits may be counterbalanced by deep-frying!). This makes a good side dish or even a nice snack for the kids after school.

- Cut the kelp into 3-inch pieces using kitchen shears.

- Pour enough vegetable oil into a small saucepan or deep skillet to cover the kelp. Heat over medium heat. Using long wooden chopsticks or tongs, carefully add the kelp one piece at a time to the oil until the pan is full with a single layer of the kelp. Cook until the kelp turns dark green and bubbles appear on the surface. Turn the pieces and cook the other side until each piece is crispy.

- Line a plate with paper towels and place the kelp on it. Sprinkle immediately with sugar while the oil is still hot. (You don't want to go crazy with the sugar, but you do want to be able to see some sugar crystals on the kelp.) Repeat with the rest of the pieces until all of them are cooked.

- Serve warm as a side dish or snack.

MAKES 4 SERVINGS

1 large sheet kelp/seaweed *(dashima)*
Vegetable oil
Sugar

chilled cucumber soup

(oi naeng-gook)

I usually use small pickling cucumbers for this dish so that I won't have to bother with peeling or seeding them. You can also use Persian or English cukes, if you can't find the smaller variety at your local market. Feel free to experiment with the vinegar, sugar, and salt until you get the broth to your liking. The sour and slightly sweet liquid is a wonderful thirst quencher for those dog days of summer.

Stir the water, vinegar, sugar, and salt together in a medium bowl until the sugar and salt are dissolved. Add the cucumbers, garlic, green onion, sesame oil, and pepper and stir. Taste the liquid and adjust the seasonings if necessary. It should have a strong flavor since the ice cubes will dilute it some.

Spoon into individual bowls. Sprinkle with toasted sesame seeds and add a few ice cubes to each serving to keep it chilled.

VARIATION:
Soak about 2 ounces dried kelp (miyeok) *in water to cover for 5 to 10 minutes. The seaweed will swell and turn dark green. Cut the kelp into pieces about 2 inches long and add to the cucumbers.*

MAKES 4 TO 6 SERVINGS

3 cups cold water
¼ cup white vinegar, plus 2 tablespoons
1 tablespoon sugar
½ teaspoon salt
2 small pickling cucumbers
  (about 4 ounces), grated
1 clove garlic, finely minced
1 green onion, chopped
1 tablespoon Asian sesame oil
1 teaspoon freshly ground white pepper
2 tablespoons toasted sesame seeds
Ice cubes

seasoned green onion salad

(pa moochim)

⎯

This salad usually would be served with thinly sliced roast beef that is cooked on a tabletop *dak gui* grill or in an electric frying pan. It makes a nice accompaniment to any grilled meat, such as *dak gui* (page 74) or *galbi* (page 79).

🍲 Cut the green onions into 2-inch lengths, then cut the pieces lengthwise into strips as thin as possible.

🍲 Toss the green onions with the lettuce in a large bowl. Add the sesame oil, vinegar, chile powder, and salt and toss. Serve immediately as a side dish.

VARIATION:
Coarsely chop 8 to 10 broad perilla leaves (or 1 bunch smaller leaves) and toss with the lettuce. Found in most Asian supermarkets, perilla leaves can also be served on the side (along with leaves of curly leaf lettuce) to use as a wrap for grilled meats.

MAKES 4 TO 6 SERVINGS

4 green onions
1 head curly leaf lettuce, shredded
3 tablespoons Asian sesame oil
2 tablespoons rice vinegar
1 teaspoon Korean chile powder
1 teaspoon salt or to taste

chicken, beef, and pork

74
Grilled Chicken
(DAK GUI)

75
Chicken Skewers with Green Onions

77
Spicy Chile Chicken
(MAE-UN DAK)

78
Seasoned Fried Chicken
(YANGNYEOM DAK)

79
Barbecued Beef Ribs
(GALBI)

81
Skewered Beef
(SANJOK)

82
Barbecued Pork Ribs
(DWEJI GALBI)

83
Seasoned Sliced Beef
(BOOLGOGI)

85
Braised Beef Ribs
(GALBI JJIM)

86
Spicy Sliced Pork
(DWEJI BOOLGOGI)

87
Soy Stewed Beef
(JANG JOLIM)

BECAUSE MOST PEOPLE'S INTRODUCTION TO KOREAN CUISINE IS through eating barbecue at restaurants, they have the mistaken belief that Koreans eat a lot of meat. Korea historically has been a poor country where meat was generally reserved for special occasions or added only as a condiment for a dish. In fact, the most famous Korean dish, *galbi* (beef short ribs), was invented in restaurants in the latter half of the twentieth century.

History aside, there are a number of fabulously tasty meat dishes enjoyed today. I've assembled a mix of traditional and modern recipes for you to try. Some of them require a little bit of planning—it's best to marinate the meats to let the flavors infuse. But once they have soaked up the spices, you can easily throw them on a grill, cook them up in a pan, or bake them in the oven.

If you do make any of these dishes for a barbecue or summer party, save a bit for yourself. When you pull yourself away from the grill, you'll be sad to find there is nothing left for you to enjoy.

grilled chicken

(dak gui)

Chicken is probably one of the most ubiquitous meats in America, but one that can be very versatile. Here's a lovely chicken dish to add to your repertoire. If you don't want to bother with a grill, you can sauté in a skillet or bake in the oven.

🌀 Rinse the chicken with cold water and blot dry with paper towels. Score the chicken with a knife, making a few shallow cuts on each piece.

🌀 Combine the onion, garlic, ginger, soy sauce, sugar, malt syrup, sesame oil, and black pepper in a large bowl. Add the chicken and turn the pieces until the chicken is covered with marinade. Cover and refrigerate for at least 2 hours (or overnight).

🌀 Preheat a gas grill to medium-low. If using a charcoal grill, make sure that the coals are just covered with white ash and the flames have died down a bit. Grill the chicken until cooked through, 20 to 30 minutes (depending on the size of the pieces), turning occasionally.

MAKES 6 TO 8 SERVINGS
3 pounds skinless chicken breasts (bone in or boneless)
½ onion, grated
2 cloves garlic, minced
One 1-inch piece ginger, minced
¼ cup soy sauce
2 tablespoons sugar
¼ cup Korean malt syrup *(mool yut)*
1 tablespoon Asian sesame oil
1 teaspoon freshly ground black pepper

chicken skewers with green onions

These kebabs are great as an appetizer or main course when you're planning an outdoor barbecue. You can also bake them in the oven, if you don't want to bother with a grill. I usually soak the skewers in cold water before I'm going to use them to keep them from burning on the grill.

- Soak 12 thin bamboo skewers in cold water for 30 to 60 minutes.

- Combine the soy sauce, garlic, ginger, sesame seeds, sugar, sesame oil, and black pepper to taste in a small bowl.

- Cut the chicken into long strips. Cut the green onions into pieces about 1½ inches long. Pierce the chicken and green onions on the skewers, alternating between the two.

- Place the skewers in a long baking dish and pour the marinade over them. Refrigerate for at least 4 hours (or overnight), turning them occasionally.

- Preheat a gas grill to medium. If using a charcoal grill, make sure that the coals are just covered with white ash and the flames have died down a bit. Cook until the chicken is cooked through, 4 to 5 minutes per side.

NOTE:
You can also marinate the chicken and green onions in a large plastic zipper bag and skewer them just before grilling.

MAKES 6 MAIN-COURSE OR
12 APPETIZER SERVINGS
2 tablespoons soy sauce
3 cloves garlic, minced
One 2-inch piece ginger, grated
2 tablespoons toasted sesame seeds
1 tablespoon sugar
1 tablespoon Asian sesame oil
Freshly ground black pepper
2 pounds boneless, skinless chicken breasts
16 green onions

spicy chile chicken
(mae-un dak)

There is a town in the Gyeonggi province of Korea that specializes in this dish. You can drive down the streets and see a chicken restaurant on practically every corner. All the joints are pretty much the same with huge, flat griddles on the table. Once you sit down, the waitresses will pile on all the ingredients, pour on the chile paste seasoning, and cook the dish right in front of you as you salivate in anticipation. You can re-create the fun at home with an electric frying pan or make it in a large skillet or wok.

Heat the oil in a large skillet or wok over high heat. Add the chicken, yam, onion, zucchini, cabbage, and garlic and stir-fry until the chicken is cooked through and the vegetables begin to brown, 15 to 20 minutes. Add the green onion, chile paste, soy sauce, and sugar and cook for a couple of minutes or so.

Serve immediately with hot rice.

VARIATION:
If you're using an electric frying pan on the table, you can keep the chicken hot as you eat from the frying pan. As you near the bottom of the dish, add leftover white rice to the pan with a bit of sesame oil and make fried rice to finish off the meal.

MAKES ABOUT 4 SERVINGS
1 tablespoon vegetable oil
1 pound skinless, boneless chicken,
    cut into about 2-inch pieces
1 yam, peeled and cut into thin strips
    about 2 inches long
1 small onion, cut into 1-inch cubes
1 zucchini, cut into 1-inch cubes
¼ head cabbage, cut into 1-inch cubes
    (about 2 cups)
2 cloves garlic, sliced
1 green onion, cut into 2-inch lengths
3 tablespoons Korean chile paste
1 teaspoon soy sauce
1 teaspoon sugar

seasoned fried chicken

(yangnyeom dak)

As American fast-food companies have begun to add their arches and colonels to the Korean culinary landscape, Koreans have added their special touch to certain dishes. This spicy fried chicken recipe is a wonderful example. It's a bit messy to eat, but your only regret will be that you didn't make more. If you don't want to cut the chicken into small pieces, ask your butcher to do it for you.

Toss the chicken with the onion and garlic and marinate for at least 30 minutes in the refrigerator.

Whisk the egg, water, cornstarch, salt, and pepper together in a medium bowl just until moist. Do not overmix.

Over medium heat, heat at least an inch of oil in a deep heavy saucepan. Using long chopsticks or tongs, dip one chicken piece at a time in the cornstarch mixture and carefully place it in the hot oil. Repeat until the pan is almost full but the chicken pieces aren't touching. Cook until crispy and golden brown, usually about 10 minutes. To check if it's cooked through, take out the largest piece and cut to see that the juices run clear. Place the pieces on a plate lined with paper towels. Repeat until all the pieces are cooked.

Mix the chile paste, sugar, ketchup, sesame seeds, and lemon juice in a large bowl. Add the fried chicken and carefully turn to coat all the pieces with the seasoning. Serve immediately.

MAKES 4 OR 5 SERVINGS

1 pound skinless, boneless chicken, cut into 2- to 3-inch pieces
½ onion, grated
1 clove garlic, minced
1 large egg
1 cup cold water
1 cup cornstarch
1 teaspoon salt
1 teaspoon freshly ground black pepper
Vegetable oil for frying
3 tablespoons Korean chile paste
5 tablespoons sugar
4 tablespoons ketchup
2 tablespoons toasted sesame seeds
Juice of ½ lemon

barbecued beef ribs

(galbi)

This is the classic dish you get when you order barbecue at a Korean restaurant. There are two cuts of beef ribs available at the Korean market. One is cut with a big hunk of bone with the meat attached (you have to slice the meat thinner). The other is sliced thinly with three rib bones attached. I usually use the latter, but feel free to use other cuts of beef, ribs, or even skirt steak (carne asada). I always got in trouble from my grandma for licking my fingers (it's considered bad manners in Korea), but try this dish and you'll be tempted to lick your fingers, too. Serve with curly leafed lettuce to wrap the meat in, steamed rice, kimchi, and your choice of side dishes.

- Mix the onion, garlic, soy sauce, sugar, pineapple juice, sesame oil, and black pepper in a medium bowl.

- Layer the meat in a shallow pan, spooning the marinade over each layer, or combine the meat with the marinade in a couple of large plastic zipper bags. Refrigerate for at least 3 hours but preferably overnight.

- Cook the meat over medium-hot coals (or over a gas grill preheated to medium) until well done and crispy on the edges, about 3 to 5 minutes on each side. If you don't want to bother with a grill, bake them in a preheated 425°F oven until browned, 10 to 12 minutes, flipping them once during cooking.

MAKES 10 TO 12 SERVINGS

1 medium onion, minced

1 bulb garlic, minced

⅓ cup soy sauce

½ cup sugar

1 cup pineapple juice

2 tablespoons Asian sesame oil

1 teaspoon freshly ground black pepper

5 pounds beef short ribs

skewered beef

(sanjok)

This is an easy but elegant dish to start off any dinner party. Traditionally *sanjok* was made for special occasions, but why worry about formalities with a dish that tastes so good? The rice cake sticks can be found fresh, frozen, or refrigerated in Korean markets, which also sell the short bamboo skewers you'll need for this dish.

⟳ Soak the short (5- or 6-inch) bamboo skewers in cold water for at least 30 minutes.

⟳ Put the beef in a medium bowl, add the soy sauce, garlic, sesame oil, sugar, and black pepper, and toss to combine, making sure all the beef is coated with the marinade. Let sit for at least 20 minutes.

⟳ Using two parallel skewers, thread the beef, green onions, and rice cakes alternately on the sticks.

⟳ Prepare a medium-hot coal fire or preheat a gas grill to medium. Grill the skewers until the meat is browned on both sides and cooked through, 3 to 4 minutes on each side.

NOTE:
Cut the green onions just a bit shorter than the length of meat, since the meat will shrink during cooking. If you don't want to bother with a grill, you can also sauté these in an large oiled skillet.

MAKES 5 OR 6 SERVINGS

1 pound tender beef, such as rib-eye or
    filet mignon, cut into thin 2-inch-long strips
1 tablespoon soy sauce
2 cloves garlic, minced
1 teaspoon Asian sesame oil
1 tablespoon sugar
1 teaspoon freshly ground black pepper
5 or 6 green onions, cut into 2-inch lengths
    (see Note)
1 package rice cake sticks
    (ddukbokgi dduk)

barbecued pork ribs
(dweji galbi)

You can use any sort of pork ribs for this dish and it'll turn out great. The chile paste and ginger add a spicy kick to the marinade. If you can't find Korean malt syrup *(mool yut)*, you can substitute about ¼ cup corn syrup (which is sweeter and not as thick) or add more sugar. This tasty dish will be the highlight of any barbecue, but be sure to save some for yourself before all your guests get to them first.

Separate the ribs and place in a large bowl.

Combine the ginger, garlic, chile paste, malt syrup, sugar, soy sauce, and sesame oil in a small bowl. Pour the marinade over the meat and turn the pieces until all the meat is coated. Cover and refrigerate for at least 2 hours but preferably overnight.

Prepare a medium-hot coal fire or preheat a gas grill to medium. Grill the pork until done, 5 to 6 minutes on each side.

NOTE:
You can also bake the ribs in a preheated 425°F oven. Line a cookie sheet with aluminum foil, lay out the ribs, and bake for 15 to 18 minutes, turning the ribs once.

MAKES 10 TO 12 SERVINGS
5 pounds pork back ribs
One 1-inch piece ginger, chopped
1 clove garlic, minced
1 cup Korean chile paste
½ cup Korean malt syrup *(mool yut)*
½ cup sugar
2 tablespoons soy sauce
3 tablespoons Asian sesame oil

seasoned sliced beef

(boolgogi)

This is a delicious dish that's super-easy to make. You can find the thinly sliced beef in Korean markets or have your butcher slice it for you. Feel free to add other vegetables to this dish. Good candidates are oyster or shiitake mushrooms, onions, zucchini, bell peppers of any color, or even thinly sliced carrots. Koreans like to use toasted sesame seeds as a garnish for many dishes, but they're not necessary if you don't happen to have any around. Serve with kimchi, steamed rice, and your choice of side dishes.

- Marinate the beef in the soy sauce, sesame oil, sugar, and garlic for about 30 minutes (or overnight if you want).

- Heat a large skillet over medium-high heat. Add the beef and stir-fry until completely browned, 5 to 7 minutes.

- Add the black pepper and green onions and cook until the green onions are slightly limp but still retain their color, 1 to 2 minutes. Sprinkle with sesame seeds if you like and serve immediately.

MAKES 5 OR 6 SERVINGS

2 pounds rib-eye or other tender beef, thinly sliced

2 tablespoons soy sauce

2 teaspoons Asian sesame oil

1 tablespoon sugar

1 bulb garlic, minced

Freshly ground black pepper to taste

3 green onions, cut into 1-inch pieces

Toasted sesame seeds for garnish

braised beef ribs

(galbi jjim)

This recipe, like all beef dishes in Korea, was usually made for parties and special occasions. Nowadays we don't have to worry about the price of beef, so we can enjoy this for an everyday meal. It's perfect with a bowl of white rice, salad, and a bit of kimchi on the side.

- Trim any excess fat from the ribs and score the meat for better marinating.

- Put the soy sauce, sugar, sesame oil, and garlic in a small bowl and stir until the sugar is dissolved.

- Put the ribs, radish, onion, carrots, and ginger in a medium, heavy-bottomed pot or Dutch oven. Pour the sauce over all and add the water. Bring to a boil. Reduce the heat and simmer uncovered for about 1 hour. The beef should be well cooked and tender; if it isn't, cook for an additional 15 minutes.

- Since short-rib meat tends to be fatty, be sure to skim the fat. Remove the ginger slices and discard. Serve hot, garnished with pine nuts.

NOTE:
If using a slow cooker, layer all the ingredients, then pour in the water. Add extra water if necessary to make sure all the ingredients are covered. Cook on high for 4 to 5 hours or low for 7 to 8 hours.

MAKES 6 OR 7 SERVINGS
3 pounds beef short ribs
1 cup soy sauce
3 tablespoons sugar
2 tablespoons Asian sesame oil
3 cloves garlic, minced
1 medium daikon radish, cut into 2-inch cubes
1 medium onion, cut into 1-inch cubes
3 carrots, cut into 1-inch-thick slices
One 2-inch piece ginger, sliced
3 cups water
Pine nuts for garnish

spicy sliced pork

(dweji boolgogi)

Thinly sliced pork loin can be found in Korean groceries, but you can ask the butcher at any market to cut it for you. This is a great dish to get on the table when you're in a hurry and don't want to fuss with dinner.

- Combine the chile paste, sugar, garlic, ginger, soy sauce, rice wine (if using), sesame oil, and pepper in a large mixing bowl. Add the pork and onion and turn to coat. Let marinate for at least 30 minutes in the refrigerator.

- Cook the pork in a large skillet over medium-high heat, stirring occasionally, until completely cooked and beginning to brown a bit.

- Serve immediately with hot rice.

NOTE:

This dish is usually served with curly leaf lettuce (either green or red) for wrapping the meat with Spicy Soybean Paste (page 157). If you're in a big hurry and don't have time to marinate, you can season and cook the pork right in the pan. The meat won't have soaked in all the flavors, but it'll still taste pretty good.

MAKES ABOUT 6 SERVINGS

3 tablespoons Korean chile paste

3 tablespoons sugar

3 cloves garlic, minced

One 1-inch piece ginger, minced

1 tablespoon soy sauce

1 tablespoon rice wine (optional)

1 tablespoon Asian sesame oil

1 teaspoon freshly ground black pepper

2 pounds pork loin, sliced as thinly as possible

1 onion, sliced (optional)

soy stewed beef

(jang jolim)

This is a good way to cook any tough cut of beef, since simmering makes the meat tender. A flavorful dish, it makes a comfortable weeknight meal.

- Put the beef brisket, radish, and the ginger in a medium, heavy-bottomed pot or Dutch oven and add the water. Bring to a boil, reduce the heat, and simmer uncovered for about 1 hour.

- Remove the meat and let cool until it's safe to touch. Shred or thinly slice the beef. Skim the fat and foam from the broth and return the beef. Add the soy sauce, sugar, garlic, and onion and simmer for about 20 minutes. Add the chiles, green onion, and eggs and simmer until the eggs are hard-boiled, 5 to 8 minutes.

- Remove the eggs and run them under cold water until they are cool to handle. Peel and cut the eggs lengthwise in half.

- Serve warm or cold as a side dish with the eggs placed on top. The sauce is nice over rice.

VARIATION:
The traditional version of this dish is made with tiny quail eggs (maechuli-al), *but since they are such a pain to peel, I use regular chicken eggs.*

MAKES 2 OR 3 SERVINGS
8 ounces beef brisket or shank
¼ small daikon radish, cut into 2-inch cubes
One 1-inch piece ginger, sliced
3 cups water
½ cup soy sauce
1 teaspoon sugar
5 cloves garlic, peeled
1 small onion, cut into 1-inch cubes
3 small Korean or other green chiles, sliced, with or without seeds
1 green onion, cut into 2-inch lengths
2 large eggs, washed

fish and shellfish

LIVING ON A PENINSULA, THE PEOPLE OF KOREA HAVE ENJOYED THE fruits of the sea for centuries. If it's from the ocean and it's edible, Koreans have probably figured out not only how to eat it but also how to enjoy the best flavors from it.

Tiny towns along the peninsula's coast are filled with places that sell raw fish *(hwae)*, spicy hot pots made from a variety of seafoods, and open markets where any manner of sea creatures are crawling or swimming in bubbling tanks. The glistening silver bodies of fresh fish and piles of shellfish invite you to take them home for dinner.

I could fill an entire volume with recipes for fish and seafood, but I've collected a sampling to get you started in your ocean-inspired culinary adventure. You can start with some Spicy Stewed Mussels (page 99), Grilled Shrimp (page 93), or even Grilled Mackerel (page 95). Enjoy the wonderful gifts from the ocean as we Koreans have for generations.

grilled shrimp

(saewoo gui)

Koreans usually eat shrimp plain, grilled, or lightly salted. I've taken the basic idea and added some spice to take the shrimp to the next level. If you're using frozen shrimp, make sure they've been defrosted and drained before marinating.

- Put the shrimp in a large bowl. Add the soy sauce, rice wine, garlic, ginger, and lime juice and combine. Sprinkle with the chile powder and toss.

- Place a grill basket or aluminum pan (or a piece of heavy-duty aluminum foil) on a preheated grill. Add the shrimp and cook, turning, until they've turned pink.

- Serve hot with rice and other side dishes.

MAKES 4 TO 6 SERVINGS

About 1 pound large shrimp,
    peeled and deveined
2 tablespoons soy sauce
1 tablespoon rice wine
2 cloves garlic, minced
One 1-inch piece ginger, minced
Juice from ½ lime
1 teaspoon Korean chile powder

egg-battered alaskan pollack

(dongtae jeon)

Battered food is usually made for *janchi* (parties) but can be enjoyed for dinner parties or as a special addition to a weekday meal. I've used Alaskan pollack in this dish because you can find it already sliced in Korean markets, but any meaty white fish, such as tilapia or cod, will do. If you buy your fish frozen, be sure it's thoroughly defrosted. But remember, if the fish is not presliced, it's easier to cut when it is still slightly frozen. I set up an assembly line and use long wooden chopsticks to dip the fish, so that my fingers don't get so gunky from the batter. And I can use the sticks to cook the fish, too.

- Beat the eggs with the salt in a small bowl as if you're going to scramble them.

- Pour a bit of flour on a large plate and spread it out. Leave the flour out since you'll need to add more as you go.

- Heat enough vegetable oil to thinly cover the bottom of a large skillet over medium heat. Working with one piece at a time, dust the fish on both sides in the flour, dip into the egg, and immediately place in the skillet. Fry the fish in a single layer until slightly browned, 3 to 4 minutes on each side.

- Serve immediately with Seasoned Soy Sauce.

MAKES 6 TO 8 SERVINGS

4 large eggs
1/8 teaspoon salt
Flour for dusting
Vegetable oil for cooking
1 pound Alaskan pollack,
    sliced about ¼ inch thick
Seasoned Soy Sauce (page 155)

grilled mackerel
(ggonchi gui)

Although I've written this recipe for mackerel, you can prepare any small fresh fish this way. Koreans, like most other Asians, aren't worried about serving the whole fish, head and all, but if you're bothered by seeing the face of the fish, cut off the head before cooking. You can find fish cleaned and gutted in the seafood section of most Asian grocers, but feel free to scale and clean your own, especially if you've caught the fish yourself.

- ⚇ If it's not prepared already, scale and clean the mackerel, removing the entrails. Depending on the size of the fish, cut four or so slits on both sides of each fish. If you prefer not to present the whole fish, you may cut the fish into four or so pieces each, leaving off the heads and tails.

- ⚇ Sprinkle the fish on both sides with salt and let sit for a few minutes.

- ⚇ In the meantime, heat a grill to medium. Cook the fish on the grill, turning once, until cooked through, 3 to 4 minutes on each side.

- ⚇ Serve immediately with lemon wedges if you wish, so that you can squeeze the juice over the fish.

NOTE:
If you don't want to bother with a grill, you can cook the fish in a skillet. Add about 1 tablespoon of oil to the pan and heat over medium-high heat. Add the fish and sauté until it's thoroughly cooked and the skin is browned and crispy, about 5 minutes on each side depending on the thickness of the fish.

MAKES ABOUT 4 SERVINGS

2 mackerel pike (1 to 2 pounds each)
About 1 tablespoon salt
Lemon wedges (optional)

spicy eel with green onions

(jang-uh gui)

This is a nice and spicy way to prepare freshwater eel (whose name in Korean literally translates to "snake eel"). Eel is one of three major dishes eaten during *Sambok* (the three hottest days of the year). The other dishes eaten during *Sambok* are red bean porridge *(pot jook)* and *samgyetang*, a healthful soup made from a whole chicken, ginseng, and other tasty ingredients. According to theories of Oriental medicine, the body may be hot but the internal organs are relatively cold. Warming up one's insides is not only a way to overcome the summer heat but also a way to fight off disease and fatigue. Whether you subscribe to these beliefs or not, this recipe is a tasty way to enjoy your eel.

- If the eel is not already prepared, clean it by cutting off the head and removing the entrails. Cut into pieces about 2 inches long.

- Heat the vegetable oil in a medium skillet over medium-high heat. Add the eel and sauté until the edges are crispy, 5 to 7 minutes. Remove to a plate lined with paper towels to drain.

- Pour off the oil in the skillet (you can use the same one). Add the sesame oil, chiles, and ginger and stir-fry for 2 minutes. Add the chile paste and sugar and cook, stirring, for about 1 minute. Add the eel and green onions to the sauce and stir until coated. Remove from the heat, sprinkle with sesame seeds, and serve with rice.

MAKES 3 OR 4 SERVINGS

1 freshwater eel

1 tablespoon vegetable oil

1 tablespoon Asian sesame oil

2 Korean chiles (red or green, but red ones will be hotter), sliced with seeds

One 1-inch piece ginger, sliced

2 tablespoons Korean chile paste

1 tablespoon sugar

3 green onions, chopped

Toasted sesame seeds for garnish

spicy stewed mussels

(Hong-ap Jjim)

In late autumn, when cold winds begin blowing down from Siberia to the Korean peninsula, the open markets are filled with fresh, inexpensive mussels gathered from nearby coasts. When choosing these lovely shellfish, look for fresh ones with closed, unchipped shells. This way of preparing these black treasures makes for a messy, spicy, finger-lickin' good main attraction or a terrific side to serve with a cold beer or *soju*.

❁ Soak the mussels in cold water to cover for about 20 minutes (they'll expel sand and salt, making them easier to clean). Remove the beards by yanking them toward the hinge end (use a dry towel to grasp them if they're slippery from the water). Remove the mussels from the water, scrub off any barnacles with a brush, and place them in a clean bowl. Don't drain or rinse them in a colander, or the sand will come along with the mussels.

❁ Pour 1 cup water into a large pot and bring to a boil. Add the mussels, cover, and let steam for 5 to 6 minutes. Stir the mussels and let steam for another 3 minutes or so. You'll know they're done when the shells open and the water becomes milky. Drain the mussels and reserve the broth.

❁ Add the oil and garlic to a large skillet or wok. Stir-fry over medium-high heat for a couple of minutes, then add the chile powder and green chile. Cook for another couple of minutes, then add the chile paste, soy sauce, and malt syrup and stir to combine. Add the reserved broth while continuing to stir, then add the mussels and toss over the heat for a couple of minutes.

❁ Serve immediately with rice and any other side dishes you like.

MAKES 4 TO 6 SERVINGS

1 pound fresh mussels

1 cup water

1 tablespoon vegetable oil

2 cloves garlic, minced

1 tablespoon Korean chile powder

1 Korean green chile, sliced with seeds

2 tablespoons Korean chile paste

2 tablespoons soy sauce

1 tablespoon Korean malt syrup *(mool yut)*

sautéed octopus
(nakji bokkeum)

Enjoyed by many Koreans, this is one of those spicy dishes that gives Korean food the (sometimes undeserved) reputation of being too hot for Western palates. An easy stir-fry to make, the octopus can be replaced with squid *(ojing-uh)* and cooked exactly the same way. It can be served next to or on top of a bed of rice.

MAKES 5 OR 6 SERVINGS

- If it's not already prepared, wash and rinse the octopus, removing any beaks and inside parts of the heads. Slice about ½-inch-thick and drain well.

- Combine the chile paste, soy sauce, sugar, chile powder, garlic, and sesame oil in a medium bowl. Add the octopus and mix to coat. Let marinate for about 10 minutes.

- Heat the vegetable oil in a large skillet or wok over medium-high heat. Add the onion, carrot, chile, and marinated octopus. Stir-fry until the octopus is cooked through (the meat will turn opaque), 8 to 10 minutes. Add the green onions and cook for about another minute.

- Serve hot, generously sprinkled with sesame seeds if desired.

1 pound fresh (or thawed if frozen) octopus,
    cut into bite-size pieces
3 tablespoons Korean chile paste
1 tablespoon soy sauce
1 tablespoon sugar
1 tablespoon Korean chile powder
2 cloves garlic, minced
2 tablespoons Asian sesame oil
1 tablespoon vegetable oil
1 medium onion, sliced
½ small carrot, thinly sliced on the diagonal
1 Korean red or green chile, sliced with seeds
3 green onions, cut into 2-inch lengths
Toasted sesame seeds for garnish (optional)

stir-fried spicy dried squid

(ojing-uh-chae bokkeum)

This easy dish is a spicy addition to any meal. The chewy texture of the dried squid makes it fun to eat. Remember that sesame oil burns easily, so watch the heat carefully.

- Soak the squid strips in cold water for about 10 minutes. Drain well.

- While the squid is soaking, combine the chile paste, soy sauce, sugar, vinegar, and garlic in a small bowl.

- Heat the sesame oil in a large skillet over medium-low heat. Add the sauce and heat for just under a minute. Add the squid strips and toss until well coated. Cook until the liquid is mostly evaporated. Serve warm or at room temperature, sprinkled with sesame seeds.

MAKES ABOUT 4 SERVINGS

4 ounces dried squid strips
4 tablespoons Korean chile paste
1 tablespoon soy sauce
1 tablespoon sugar
1 teaspoon rice vinegar
1 clove garlic, minced
1 tablespoon Asian sesame oil
Sesame seeds for garnish

kimchi and other pickled things

EVERY AUTUMN THE OUTDOOR MARKETS OF KOREA ARE FILLED WITH the bounties of the harvest. Fresh vegetables and fruits from the peninsula's fertile river plains make their way to open markets in winding alleyways and eventually onto the dining tables of families throughout the country.

In more agricultural times, the seasonal kimchi making (called *gimjang*) was a communal affair that took at least a couple of days. Groups of women would flock to someone's home and convert piles of cabbages, green onions, and garlic into rows of jars filled with the spicy pickled stuff of Korean legend. The owner of the house would make sure she fed those friends and relatives during those couple of days of chopping, slicing, mincing, and working. Helping their friends, family, and neighbors prepare the harvest for the coming winter, everyone would make their rounds.

When I was growing up, it seemed everyone came to our house to make kimchi. Each woman would take home a jar or two for her labor. It was a time for loud talking, gossiping, and laughing, while our hands were covered with the garlicky red stuff that makes kimchi taste so good.

Women of my generation don't make kimchi. We rarely have time to get together a couple of times a year, let alone spend a whole day peeling garlic and chopping vegetables, but kimchi making doesn't have to be such a labor-intensive affair. You'll need a large glass jar, a good knife, and the desire to enjoy the mouthwatering reward once you've waited patiently for your batch to be ready.

quick kimchi
(mak gimchi)

Although a bit of prep work is required, you can have your very own homemade kimchi with minimal effort. This is a variation of the most popular variety, the traditional *baechu* (napa cabbage) kimchi. You might think that a gallon is a lot of kimchi, but you can use leftovers to make Kimchi Pancakes (page 37) or Kimchi Fried Rice (page 122) or even put it into your Thanksgiving stuffing. You'll need a 1-gallon glass jar with a tight-fitting lid.

- Rinse the cabbages and cut them crosswise into about 2-inch lengths. Peel the daikon, cut lengthwise into quarters, then into pieces about ½ inch thick.

- Dissolve the salt in 1 cup water. Put the cabbages and daikon in a large bowl and pour the salt water over them. Let sit at least 6 hours or overnight.

- The next day, drain the vegetables but reserve the water. Return the cabbages and daikon to the same bowl. Add the green onions, garlic, ginger, chile powder, and fish sauce and mix well. Pack the mixture into a 1-gallon glass jar. Slowly pour the reserved salty water over the vegetables to cover, leaving about 1 inch of space on top. Tightly close the jar.

- Let the jar sit in a cool, dark place for 2 to 3 days, depending on the weather and how ripe (pickled) you like your kimchi. Refrigerate after opening. It will keep for a couple of weeks, after which you'll want to make fried rice, kimchi pancakes, or a hot pot with it.

NOTE:
Traditionally, baechu *kimchi was made with tiny salted shrimp (available in small jars in the refrigerated section of Korean markets), which you can use in place of the fish sauce. I've discovered that fish sauce is more versatile and easier to find than salted shrimp. Any brand of the Asian fish sauce will do.*

MAKES ABOUT 1 GALLON

2 napa cabbages
1 medium daikon radish
¼ cup coarse sea salt
1 cup water
4 green onions, cut into 2-inch lengths
7 cloves garlic, minced
2 tablespoons minced or grated ginger
2 tablespoons Korean chile powder
2 tablespoons Asian fish sauce

daikon kimchi

(ggakdoogi)

This is a nice kimchi to have around, especially in the summer. The crispy radish is an excellent addition to any meal, especially one in which you're serving meat. If the kimchi is not fully ripe (pickled), sprinkle it with a bit of sesame oil and sesame seeds on top. You will need a 1-gallon jar with a tight-fitting lid.

- Put the garlic, ginger, chile powder, salt, and sugar in a food processor and pulse until finely minced. If you don't have a processor or don't want to bother, just mince the garlic and ginger with a large knife, then combine with the chile powder, salt, and sugar.

- Put the daikon and mustard greens in a large bowl and mix with the garlic seasoning until all the daikon is nice and red.

- Pack the vegetables into a 1-gallon glass jar and close tightly. Let the jar sit in a cool, dark place for 3 to 4 days, depending on the weather (kimchi ferments faster in warmer weather). Refrigerate after opening. It will keep a couple of weeks in the refrigerator.

VARIATION:

If you can't find mustard greens, you can substitute green onions. The taste will be different, but you'll at least get some additional color in your dish. Go ahead and add another tablespoon of chile powder if you like your kimchi extra spicy.

MAKES ABOUT 1 GALLON

1 bulb garlic, cloves peeled and trimmed
One 2-inch piece ginger, sliced
2 tablespoons Korean chile powder
2 tablespoons coarse sea or kosher salt
2 tablespoons sugar
2 large daikon radishes, peeled and
    cut into 1-inch cubes
1 bunch mustard greens, cut into
    1-inch lengths

water kimchi

(dongchimi)

A chilled kimchi made from small ponytail radishes or huge cubes of daikon, this is a perfect pickled dish for those who prefer foods that aren't spicy. Although traditionally made in the winter, it is a lovely addition to any summer meal. It is called water kimchi because it's served with its pickling liquid. The liquid can also be used as a base for some tasty noodles. Both types of radishes can be found in Asian groceries. Look for radishes with firm skins that are heavy for their size (that means they're nice and juicy). You'll need a 1-gallon glass jar with a tight-fitting lid.

- Rinse the radishes and cut off the stems. If you're using ponytail radishes, save the green tops for later. If using daikons, cut them into chunky 1-inch cubes. Sprinkle about 1 cup of the salt on a flat tray or in a shallow bowl and roll each wet radish in the salt, coating them well. Place them in a 1-gallon jar and add just enough water to cover. Close the jar tightly. Let sit for 2 to 3 days in a cool, dark place. Remove the radishes, reserving the salt water.

- Put the green onions, mustard greens, and chiles in a bowl and sprinkle them with ½ cup salt. Mix and let sit for about 30 minutes.

- Put the radishes, ginger, garlic, and greens mixture in the same jar. Add the tops from the ponytail radishes if using. Dissolve the sugar in 2 cups water and pour over the vegetables. Then pour the reserved salt water into the jar, making sure that the radishes are completely covered but leaving about 2 inches of space at the top of the jar (the kimchi will expand as it ferments). Close the jar tightly and let sit in a cool, dark place for 3 to 4 days. Refrigerate after opening. It will keep for more than 2 weeks in the refrigerator.

- When the kimchi is ready to serve, place some radishes and some greens in a bowl and ladle out some liquid from the jar (dilute it with a bit of cold water if it's too salty). You can also serve it with a few ice cubes.

MAKES ABOUT 1 GALLON

1 pound Asian radishes, ponytail or daikon
1½ cups coarse sea or kosher salt
4 green onions, cut into 1½-inch lengths
8 ounces mustard greens, cut into about
    1½-inch lengths
3 small green or red Korean chiles (whole)
One 2-inch piece ginger, sliced
3 cloves garlic, sliced
1 teaspoon sugar
2 cups water

VARIATION:

The traditional way of making this includes adding an Asian pear to the mix. You can peel it, remove the seeds, cut it into chunky cubes or flat squares, and add it to the jar before you pour in the salt water.

cucumber kimchi

(oi gimchi)

A popular kimchi enjoyed in the summer, this dish is a good example of the ying and the yang in Korean cuisine. The coolness of the cucumbers is balanced with the spiciness of the chile powder. Even in the fermentation process, the cucumbers stay nice and crisp. You'll need a ½-gallon glass jar to hold the cucumbers.

- Cut the cucumbers lengthwise into quarters and place in a large bowl. Dissolve the table salt in 4 cups of the water and pour over the cucumbers. Soak the cucumbers for about 20 minutes.

- Combine the garlic, onion, Korean leeks, green onions, chile powder, and sea salt in another large bowl.

- Remove the cucumbers from the salt water and rinse. Add the cucumbers to the spicy mixture and mix until the cucumbers are all well coated. Stuff the cucumbers into a ½-gallon glass jar, pressing firmly until filled.

- Dissolve the sugar in the remaining ⅓ cup water and pour over the cucumbers. Cover tightly. Let sit in a cool, dark place for 2 to 3 days before opening to see if it's ripe. The cucumbers should be sour and have absorbed the salt and flavors of the seasoning. Refrigerate after opening. It will keep for almost 2 weeks in the refrigerator.

MAKES ABOUT ½ GALLON

10 pickling cucumbers, just over a pound

⅓ cup table salt

4⅓ cups water

6 cloves garlic, minced

½ onion, diced

½ bunch Korean leeks *(buchu)*,
    cut into ½-inch lengths

5 green onions, cut into ½-inch lengths

¼ cup Korean chile powder

1 tablespoon coarse sea or kosher salt

1 teaspoon sugar

pickled peppers

(gochu jang-ajji)

Jang-ajji is another type of pickling process used in Korea, but instead of using salt as the main preservative, vegetables are suspended in a soy-sauce-and-vinegar-based liquid. It is really easy to prepare; you just have to be patient and wait for the peppers to be pickled and ready. These savory peppers can be eaten whole or sliced and served on the side with rice. You'll need a ½-gallon jar for them.

↻ Rinse the peppers and place them in a ½-gallon glass jar. Pour in the soy sauce and vinegar.

↻ Combine the water and sugar and stir until the sugar is dissolved. Slowly pour over the peppers.

↻ Tightly cover the jar and store in a cool, dry, dark place for about 2 weeks. You can serve the peppers at room temperature or chilled. Refrigerate after opening. The peppers will keep in the refrigerator for more than a couple of months.

MAKES ABOUT ½ GALLON

1 pound Korean green peppers
¾ cup soy sauce
¾ cup white or rice vinegar
¾ cup water
2 tablespoons sugar

pickled garlic

(maneul jang-ajji)

Pickled garlic can be eaten on the side with rice or added to any number of meat dishes.

- Cut the top off each garlic bulb, so that the tops of the cloves are exposed. Place the garlic in a 1-quart glass jar.

- Combine the soy sauce, vinegar, and sugar in a medium bowl and stir until the sugar is completely dissolved. Slowly pour over the garlic, then add just enough water so that all the garlic is completely immersed. Cover tightly and let sit for 2 to 3 weeks in a cool, dry, dark place.

- Serve either chilled or at room temperature. Refrigerate after opening. It will keep in the refrigerator for about 2 months.

MAKES ABOUT 20 SERVINGS

10 bulbs garlic
½ cup soy sauce
½ cup rice or white vinegar
2 tablespoons sugar

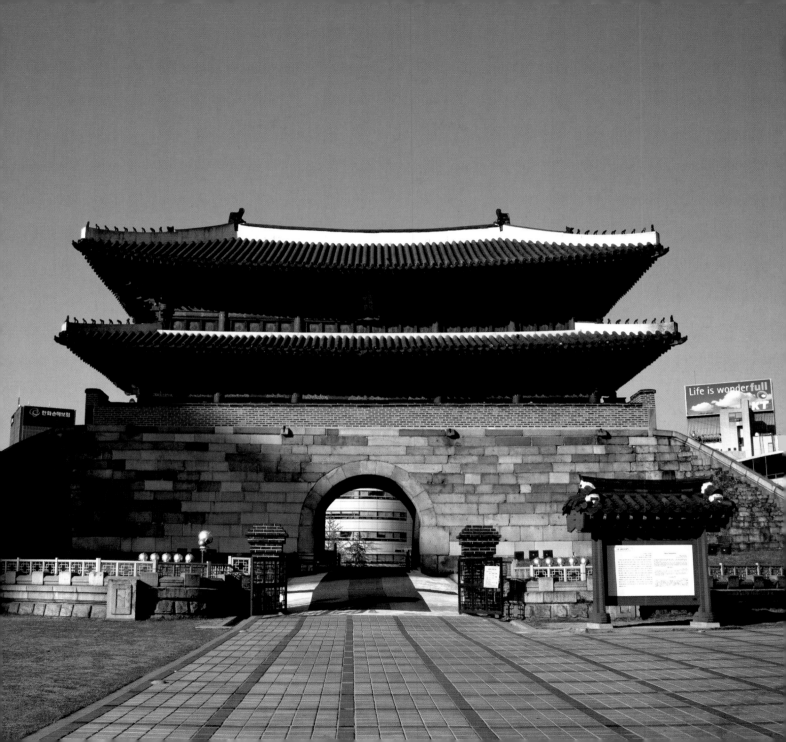

rice

119
Mixed Rice Bowl
(BIBIMBAP)

120
Red Bean Rice
(POT BAP)

121
Bean Sprout Rice Bowl
(KOHNG NAMOOL BAP)

122
Kimchi Fried Rice
(GIMCHI BOKKEUM BAP)

123
Spicy Sashimi Rice
(HWAE DUP BAP)

124
Curry Rice
(KALEH RICEUH)

125
Seaweed Rice Rolls
(GIMBAP)

RICE IS THE STAPLE OF KOREAN CUISINE. THE RICE-GROWING REGIONS of the country are the most prosperous because the white grain is the basis for most meals. Koreans even have different words for the uncooked short grains *(ssal)* and the cooked rice *(bap)*.

In any meal that isn't based on noodles, each person gets an individual bowl of rice (usually in a steel bowl with a lid). The rice serves as a base for all the side dishes that you'll enjoy with the meal.

In the next few pages I've included a variety of recipes, most of which can serve as a meal in and of themselves. Dishes such as Mixed Rice Bowl (page 119) or Spicy Sashimi Rice (page 123) can serve as elegant courses for a dinner party or a lovely weekday lunch. However you want to enjoy the dishes, feel free to experiment and add your own touches. There are no rights and wrongs in cooking, just adventures in eating.

mixed rice bowl

(bibimbap)

I'm giving you a vegetarian version of this popular dish, but all you need to make it good for omnivores is to add a bit of *boolgogi* (page 83). There are so many variations of the recipe—all depending on region, preferences, and seasons—that there is no one way of making it. So feel free to experiment with different vegetables and meats and make this recipe your very own. When I make this dish, I do the chopping and cutting first, then cook everything in succession in the same pan (fewer dishes to do later), and then assemble the bowls. All the parts can be at room temperature, but the rice should be fresh and hot.

Bring about ¼ inch water to a boil in a large pot. Add the spinach, cover, and steam until the leaves are just wilted, about 2 minutes. Immediately transfer to a colander and rinse with cold water. Squeeze the water from the spinach. Combine with the sesame oil, garlic, and salt. Set aside.

Heat the oil in a medium skillet over medium-high heat. Add the mushrooms and garlic and sauté until the mushrooms are limp and just starting to brown, about 3 minutes. Remove from the heat. Season with salt, toss, and set aside.

Using the same skillet, heat the oil over medium-high heat. Add the carrots and sauté until the carrots just turn limp, about 3 minutes. Remove from the heat. Season with salt, toss, and set aside.

Spoon 1 cup rice into each of 5 serving bowls. Arrange the cooked vegetables and grated cucumbers on top of the rice, dividing them evenly. Spoon 1 teaspoon sesame oil over each serving and pass the Seasoned Chile Paste for each person to add their own.

VARIATIONS:
You can add any number of other vegetables to this dish, including soybean sprouts, zucchini, fern bracken, shredded lettuce, or even daikon sprouts. To make it extra fancy, top each bowl with a fried egg.

MAKES 5 SERVINGS

SPINACH
2 bunches spinach (about 8 ounces),
    trimmed and well rinsed
1 tablespoon Asian sesame oil
1 clove garlic, minced
½ teaspoon salt

MUSHROOMS
1 tablespoon vegetable oil
10 shiitake or other mushrooms,
    trimmed and sliced
1 clove garlic, minced
½ teaspoon salt

CARROTS
1 tablespoon vegetable oil
2 medium carrots, grated
½ teaspoon salt

FOR SERVING
5 cups hot cooked rice
2 pickling cucumbers, grated
5 teaspoons Asian sesame oil
Seasoned Chile Paste (page 156)

red bean rice
(pot bap)

This rice can be made in place of regular white rice and is particularly nice for serving to guests. Not only is it more nutritious, but it also looks great since the beans turn the rice purple.

- Soak the red beans in cold water overnight (or start in the morning if you're planning to make it for dinner). Drain and reserve the water. Add enough additional water to measure 2¼ cups.

- Put the red beans, rice, and water in a rice cooker. Let your rice cooker do its thing. If you don't have a rice cooker, use a medium pot with a heavy bottom and a tight-fitting lid. Cover tightly and bring the rice, beans, and water to a boil. Reduce the heat to medium and simmer for about 15 minutes. Reduce the heat to low and cook for another 10 minutes. Turn off the heat and let sit covered for about 15 minutes, so the moisture can be absorbed into the grains. Serve hot and steaming in individual bowls.

NOTE:

If you forgot to soak the beans beforehand, simmer them for about 20 minutes in 1 cup water. Reserve the water and follow the instructions above.

MAKES ABOUT 4 SERVINGS

½ cup dried red beans
2 cups short-grain rice

bean sprout rice bowl

(kohng namool bap)

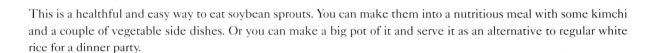

This is a healthful and easy way to eat soybean sprouts. You can make them into a nutritious meal with some kimchi and a couple of vegetable side dishes. Or you can make a big pot of it and serve it as an alternative to regular white rice for a dinner party.

🍲 Rinse the rice and place it in a rice cooker. Add the water and follow directions for your particular cooker. When the button pops up, add the soybean sprouts on top and quickly close the lid. Let steam for about 15 minutes.

🍲 Serve hot with Seasoned Soy Sauce, kimchi, and whatever *banchan* you wish.

NOTE:

If you don't have a rice cooker, cook the rice in a medium pot with a heavy bottom and a tight-fitting lid. First bring the rice and water to a boil. Reduce the heat to medium and simmer for about 15 minutes. Reduce the heat to low and cook for another 10 minutes. Turn off the heat, add the sprouts, and let sit covered for about 15 minutes, letting the steam cook the sprouts.

MAKES 5 OR 6 SERVINGS

3 cups short-grain rice
3 cups water
8 ounces soybean sprouts, rinsed
Seasoned Soy Sauce (page 155)

kimchi fried rice

(gimchi bokkeum bap)

When you have leftover rice and leftover kimchi, what do you do? I don't know about you, but I usually make fried rice. Because fried rice works best with cold rice, nothing could be easier. I usually like to add pork, since it tastes best with kimchi, but feel free to add beef, chicken, or leave the meat out altogether.

Heat the vegetable oil in a large skillet or wok over high heat. Add the onion and pork and cook until the onion is browned and the pork is cooked through, 5 to 7 minutes. Lower the heat to medium, add the butter and sesame oil, and heat until the butter melts. Add the rice and cook, stirring, over medium heat until the grains are no longer hard, 6 to 8 minutes. Add the green onions and kimchi with its liquid and cook until the green onions are limp but still retain their color, about 3 minutes. Add salt to taste and serve immediately.

VARIATION:

If you like, you can fry a couple of eggs sunny-side up and top each dish with an egg.

MAKES 2 SERVINGS

1 tablespoon vegetable oil
½ medium onion, chopped
4 ounces pork loin, chopped
1 tablespoon butter
1 tablespoon Asian sesame oil
3 cups cooked short-grain rice, chilled
2 green onions, chopped
1 cup kimchi, coarsely chopped,
    with its liquid
Salt

spicy sashimi rice

(hwae dup bap)

This one-bowl meal is a great way to enjoy your sushi fish. I like to use tilapia, salmon, and tuna, but feel free to use any raw fish you like. Super-easy to make, it can be enjoyed as a casual meal or dressed up for guests. The Vinegar Chile Sauce *(cho gochujang)* can be mighty spicy (and it's the kind of spice that sneaks up on you), so keep tasting and adding as you go.

꽃 Spoon 1 cup freshly cooked rice into each of 4 large bowls. Top with the lettuce and arrange the carrot, cucumbers, perilla, and daikon over the lettuce. Add the fish and spoon the *masago* on top.

꽃 Sprinkle a little sesame oil over each bowl and serve immediately with Vinegar Chile Sauce.

VARIATION:

If you like it extra spicy, you can also add a few slices of jalapeño or green Korean chile and/or raw garlic slices to each bowl as well.

MAKES 4 SERVINGS

4 cups hot cooked short-grain rice

6 leaves red leaf lettuce, shredded or sliced

½ carrot, julienned or coarsely grated

2 Persian or pickling cucumbers,
    julienned or coarsely grated

4 perilla leaves *(ggetnip)*, thinly sliced

½ cup julienned or coarsely grated
    daikon radish

6 ounces sushi-grade fish, sliced

4 teaspoons *masago* (smelt roe, optional)

Asian sesame oil

Vinegar Chile Sauce (page 156)

curry rice

(kaleh riceuh)

This is one of those easy dishes to make when you're not in much of a mood to cook. Since you make this in one pot, it's also a cinch to clean up afterward. It makes a nice meal for the whole family on those cold winter nights when you want something warm in your tummy. I also find it a great dish to make on camping trips when you have a hungry troop to feed. The convenient curry sauces, which come in small bricks, are available in any Asian market and come in a range of mild to spicy. Serve it with Quick Kimchi (page 107) or *ggakdoogi* (Daikon Kimchi, page 108).

Heat the oil in a large pot over high heat. Add the meat and stir-fry until the meat is browned but not necessarily cooked through, 3 to 4 minutes. Add the onion, potato, carrots, and zucchini and sauté until the onion is translucent and just beginning to brown, 3 to 4 minutes.

Pour in the water, cover, and bring to a boil. Reduce the heat and simmer until the potato is tender, about 15 minutes. Break the curry sauce bricks into pieces, add to the stew, and stir until completely dissolved. Add the peas and simmer for about 5 minutes.

Serve immediately over hot rice.

VARIATIONS:
Instead of beef, you can use any kind of meat you like (such as chicken, pork, or shrimp) or leave it out for a vegetarian version. You can also add a variety of other vegetables, including bell peppers, any type of mushroom, frozen corn, or even okra.

MAKES 10 TO 12 SERVINGS

2 tablespoons vegetable oil

1 pound stewing beef, cubed

1 medium onion, cubed

1 large potato, scrubbed or peeled and cubed

2 medium carrots, cut into thick slices

1 Korean or Italian zucchini, cubed

6 cups water

One 8- to 9-ounce package curry sauce bricks

1 cup frozen peas

10 cups hot cooked rice

seaweed rice rolls
(gimbap)

In Korea *gimbap* (which literally means "seaweed" and "rice") is picnic food. When we were growing up, our mothers would make special rolls for us whenever we went on school field trips. Nowadays *gimbap* is sold as a convenient and inexpensive street food. You can pretty much roll anything inside the rice and seaweed, but here's one of my favorite ways to make them. Pickled radish and fish sausages can be found in the refrigerated section of Asian markets. I recommend getting a bamboo rolling mat (available in most Asian markets). It will set you back only a couple of bucks and will make you the *gimbap* master you were meant to be. To save time, put the rice on to cook while you cut the ingredients.

- Cut the cucumber, sausages, and radish into long strips about ¼ inch thick.

- Stir the vinegar, sugar, and salt together in a small bowl until the sugar is dissolved. Let the rice cool slightly, then add the vinegar mixture and toss lightly.

- Set out all the ingredients and a bowl of cold water before you begin. On a flat surface or cutting board, place a sheet of *gim* on a bamboo roller. Spoon on the rice, shaping it and pressing it down to conform to the square sheet, leaving about one-third of the sheet (the part away from you) uncovered. Add a bit of radish, cucumber, and sausage in rows, starting from the edge closest to you. Wrap the roll away from you, curling your fingers and squeezing as you roll and pulling the bamboo roller from under as you go. When you're done, dip your finger in water and run it along the edge of the seaweed to seal it. Brush the outside of the roll with a bit of sesame oil. Repeat until you have used all the rice and ingredients.

- To cut the rolls, dip a large chef's knife (don't use a serrated blade), in cold water and cut slices about ¾ inch thick. Serve at room temperature with some slices of yellow pickled radish if you wish.

MAKES ABOUT 5 LIGHT LUNCH SERVINGS

1 small pickling cucumber
2 fish sausages or other mild-flavored sausage
⅛ yellow pickled radish *(danmuji)*
2 tablespoons rice or white vinegar
1 tablespoon sugar
1 teaspoon salt
3 cups hot cooked short-grain rice
5 sheets toasted laver/seaweed *(gim)*
Asian sesame oil

VARIATIONS:
You can also put cooked spinach, carrots, crabmeat, ground beef, tuna, kimchi, strips of fried eggs, or any number of things in your rolls. Feel free to experiment and find the combination you like best.

NOTE:
These rolls don't keep, so make them no earlier than the morning you intend to eat them. If you have any left over, you can freeze them and later make them into fried rice by cooking them in a skillet with a bit of oil.

noodles

LIKE ALL ASIAN CUISINES, KOREAN NOODLES HAVE THEIR ORIGINS in Chinese cuisine, but Koreans took the noodle idea and ran with it. There is a wide variety of noodles found in the Korean kitchen, everything from the college-staple ramen to handmade "knife" noodles *(kal gooksu)*.

Large bowls of noodles are usually served as a meal, replacing rice. The only exception to this are Sweet Potato Noodles (page 131), which are served as a side dish on special occasions but also make a lovely snack.

From chewy buckwheat noodles *(naengmyeon)* to thin somen noodles, Koreans love their noodles—hot, cold, mixed with spices, sometimes in soups, and every which way you can imagine. Sometimes considered a "fast food" by Korean standards, a large bowl of noodles often serves as a quick and inexpensive lunch.

Some of the most popular Korean noodle recipes take too long to fit into the quick-and-easy category. But I've included more than a handful here that are easy to make, delicious to eat, and don't require too many unusual ingredients.

One more thing: Koreans don't consider it rude to slurp one's noodles. So if you're enjoying a large bowl of some *gooksu*, don't be shy about diving right in. Everyone else will be too busy slurping from their own bowls to notice.

sweet potato noodles

(japchae)

Japchae is traditionally made for parties or celebrations, but I like to make it for a light lunch or part of a big dinner. Dried sweet potato noodles can be found in most Asian supermarkets. They are incredibly chewy but healthful and delicious. This recipe works as a side dish *(banchan)* or can even be served as an appetizer or light snack.

Cook the sweet potato noodles in a large pot of boiling water for 4 to 5 minutes. Immediately drain and rinse thoroughly under cold water. Be sure not to overcook the noodles, or they will lose their chewy texture. If you like, cut the noodles with scissors into 6- to 7-inch lengths for easier eating.

Blanch the spinach in boiling water. Rinse immediately under cold water, squeeze the water from the leaves and form into a ball, and then cut the ball in half. Combine the spinach, half the garlic, ½ teaspoon of the sesame oil, and ¼ teaspoon salt in a small bowl. Set aside to let the flavors soak in.

Heat the vegetable oil in a large skillet over medium-high heat. Add the beef, the remaining garlic, 1 teaspoon of the soy sauce, and 1 teaspoon of the sesame oil. Stir-fry until the beef is cooked, 3 to 4 minutes. Add the onion, mushrooms, and carrot and cook until the onion is translucent, about 3 minutes. Add the green onions and stir-fry for another minute. Remove from the heat.

In a large bowl, thoroughly combine the noodles, beef mixture, spinach, remaining ¼ cup soy sauce, 1 tablespoon sesame oil, and the sugar. Serve warm, sprinkled with sesame seeds.

MAKES 4 OR 5 SERVINGS

8 ounces sweet potato noodles
½ bunch spinach (about 4 ounces),
 rinsed and trimmed
2 cloves garlic, minced
1 tablespoon plus 1½ teaspoons
 Asian sesame oil
¼ teaspoon salt
1 tablespoon vegetable oil
6 ounces beef rib-eye,
 cut into ¼- to ½-inch-thick strips
¼ cup plus 1 teaspoon soy sauce
¼ medium onion, sliced
3 to 4 *pyongo* or shiitake mushrooms, sliced
1 carrot, shredded or cut into thin strips
3 green onions, cut into 1-inch pieces
¼ cup sugar
Toasted sesame seeds for garnish

noodles with chicken

(dahk kal gooksu)

Kal gooksu, which literally means "knife noodles," are so named because traditionally these noodles were cut by hand with a knife. They are thin and wide, soft and chewy, and are usually made from wheat and dusted with flour to keep the strands from sticking together. The flour has the added bonus of thickening the broth once the noodles are cooked. I don't know anyone (except for a lady who owns a noodle shop in Los Angeles) who makes these by hand anymore. The rest of us just go to the refrigerated section of the Korean market to get our noodles. This chicken version makes a nice winter meal, especially if you're feeling a bit under the weather.

- Measure the water into a large pot and bring to a boil. Add the chicken and boil over medium heat until thoroughly cooked, 20 to 25 minutes. Carefully remove the chicken and let cool.

- Add the noodles and zucchini to the boiling water and cook until the noodles are chewy, about 5 minutes. Remove from the heat and add salt and pepper to taste.

- Divide the noodles and broth among 4 large bowls. Shred or cut the chicken into thin strips and add to the bowls.

- Serve immediately with Seasoned Soy Sauce. Add the seasoning as you eat.

VARIATIONS:
This is a bare-bones version of the dish, but you can add any number of other vegetables. Some good options are sliced onions, mushrooms, grated carrots, bean sprouts, and peas.

MAKES 4 SERVINGS

1 gallon water
1 skinless whole chicken breast
   (bone in or boneless)
1 pound *kal gooksu* (knife noodles)
1 medium zucchini, grated
   or cut into thin strips
Salt
Freshly ground black pepper
Seasoned Soy Sauce (page 155)

black bean noodles

(jjajangmyeon)

Koreans will tell you this is a Chinese dish, and Chinese will tell you this is a Korean dish. The origin is clearly Chinese. In fact Chinese immigrants brought the noodles to Korea, and they were first served at a restaurant in Incheon (in Gyeonggi province, just outside of Seoul). But the *jjajangmyeon* that Koreans enjoy is a bit different from the original. Usually you'll find the dish in Korean-Chinese restaurants, but here I show you how to make it at home. The black bean sauce (*jjajang*) can be found in the refrigerated section of Korean markets.

❀ Bring a large pot of water to a boil. Drop the noodles into the boiling water and cook until the noodles are chewy, about 5 minutes. Drain and divide among 4 large bowls.

❀ Heat the oil in a wok or deep skillet over medium-high heat. Add the garlic, ginger, and onion and sauté for about 1 minute. Add the pork and cook until the pork begins to brown. Add the black bean sauce and cook for 2 to 3 minutes (taking care not to burn it). Then add the zucchini and carrot and stir-fry for 2 to 3 minutes.

❀ Stir the water, sugar, and cornstarch together in a small bowl until the sugar is dissolved. Add the cornstarch mixture to the wok. Reduce the heat a bit and simmer, stirring, until the zucchini and carrot are cooked through and the sauce thickens, 5 to 6 minutes.

❀ Ladle the sauce over the noodles, dividing it equally. Garnish with a bit of grated cucumber and serve immediately.

VARIATIONS:
You can add a small potato (cut into small cubes) or a bit of cabbage (chopped) along with the zucchini and carrot if you wish. Also beef, chicken, or even shrimp can be substituted for the pork. Garnish the bowls with daikon sprouts instead of the shredded cucumber. And the sauce is also good over rice instead of noodles.

MAKES 4 SERVINGS

1 pound *kal gooksu* (knife noodles)
¼ cup vegetable oil
2 cloves garlic, minced
One 1-inch piece ginger, minced
1 small onion, cut into ½-inch cubes
4 ounces pork loin, chopped
¼ cup Korean black bean sauce
1 zucchini, cut into ½-inch cubes
1 carrot, cut into ½-inch cubes (optional)
½ cup water
2 teaspoons sugar
2 tablespoons cornstarch
1 pickling cucumber, grated, for garnish

spicy buckwheat noodles

(bibim naengmyeon)

Korean spicy food has the kind of heat that sneaks up on you. This noodle dish is no exception. You might start eating and think that it's not so bad, but the spice builds up in your mouth until you're ready to cry "Uncle!" This dish is often served in restaurants with a bowl of plain beef broth on the side, since slices of beef are served on top of the noodles. The broth doesn't help cool down the spice, however; in fact, it actually aggravates it. I prefer to have a large glass of ice water nearby and some cucumber slices to cool me down. These super-chewy noodles can be found in the frozen or refrigerated sections or in the dried noodle aisle of Korean groceries.

Bring a large pot of water to a boil. Add the noodles and cook the dried noodles for 3 to 5 minutes or the frozen or refrigerated noodles for 2 minutes, taking care not to overcook them. Rinse under cold water and drain.

Divide the noodles equally among 4 bowls. Top each bowl with some cucumber and half of a hard-boiled egg. Serve with Vinegar Chile Sauce, letting each person add as much or as little of it as they would like and mixing as they eat.

VARIATIONS:

If you want to add a bit of sliced beef on top of each bowl of noodles, feel free to do so. To make it fancy, you can also top the dish with slices of Asian pear.

MAKES 4 SERVINGS

2 pounds Korean buckwheat noodles
(naengmyeon)
1 small pickling cucumber, grated or julienned
2 large eggs, hard-boiled, peeled, and halved
Vinegar Chile Sauce (page 156)

vegetable mixed noodles

(yachae gooksu)

Nothing beats a bowl of noodles with tasty vegetables for a quick and healthful meal. This particular recipe is great for a summer lunch, since it can be served chilled or at room temperature. I prepare the veggies while the water is coming to a boil, so I can make a tasty dish in no time.

- Bring a large pot of water to a boil. Salt the water, then add the somen and cook until al dente, 3 to 4 minutes. Rinse under cold water. Drain well and divide the noodles among 4 large bowls.

- Heat 1 tablespoon vegetable oil in a large skillet over high heat. Add the garlic and carrots and cook for 2 to 3 minutes. Add the zucchini and a little more oil if needed. Cook, stirring occasionally, until the zucchini is just slightly browned. Turn off the heat, add the green onions, and toss.

- Stir the soy sauce, sesame oil, and sugar together in a small bowl until the sugar is dissolved.

- Pile the vegetable mixture on the noodles and drizzle with the soy mixture. Top with the cucumbers, sesame seeds, and black pepper. Serve immediately.

VARIATIONS:
If you're feeling more adventurous, experiment with other vegetables. Mushrooms, onions, bell peppers, and sprouts work well.

MAKES 4 SERVINGS

Salt
1 pound dried somen noodles
(about 4 bundles)
1 tablespoon vegetable oil,
plus more if needed
2 cloves garlic, minced
3 carrots, coarsely shredded
3 small zucchini, thinly sliced crosswise
3 green onions, coarsely chopped
⅓ cup soy sauce
2 tablespoons Asian sesame oil
1½ tablespoons sugar
2 pickling or Persian cucumbers,
coarsely shredded
Toasted sesame seeds for garnish
Freshly ground black pepper (optional)

killer spicy mixed noodles

(bibim gooksu)

Koreans eat this spicy noodle dish as a quick lunch when they're in a hurry or don't want to bother with a fancy meal. I have to warn you that the sauce is quite spicy. So if you can't handle the fire, opt for one of the other somen dishes in this chapter, such as the Vegetable Mixed Noodles (page 137) or Feast Noodles (page 139). These killer noodles are usually served cold or at room temperature.

Bring a large pot of water to a boil. Salt the water, then add the somen and cook until al dente, about 3 to 4 minutes. Rinse under cold water. Drain well and divide the noodles among 4 large bowls.

Combine the chile paste, sesame oil, sugar, vinegar, and garlic in a small bowl. Add the chile sauce to the noodles and mix until coated (best to use your hands).

Divide the kimchi amoung the 4 bowls of noodles. Top with the cucumber and sprinkle with sesame seeds. Serve immediately.

VARIATION:
If you want, add half a hard-boiled egg and/or chopped red leaf lettuce to each bowl as well.

MAKES 4 SERVINGS

Salt

1 pound dried somen noodles
(about 4 bundles)

3 tablespoons Korean chile paste
(gochujang)

3 tablespoons Asian sesame oil

3 tablespoons sugar

2 teaspoons white or rice vinegar

2 cloves garlic, minced

1 cup napa cabbage *(baechu)* kimchi,
coarsely chopped, with its liquid

2 pickling or Persian cucumbers,
coarsely grated

Toasted sesame seeds for garnish

feast noodles

(janchi gooksu)

From the name of this dish, you would think that it would be a party in and of itself, but don't let the name fool you. It comes from a time when a family would have to cook enough food to feed an entire village for a *janchi* (feast). This humble noodle dish was one way to satisfy a lot of guests without breaking the bank. When Koreans ran into friends or neighbors who were unmarried, they would greet them by asking, "When are you going to treat me to *janchi gooksu?*" Although most Koreans have weddings in hotels and banquet halls these days, the dish reminds everyone of simpler times.

- Bring a large pot of water to a boil. Salt the water, then add the somen and cook until al dente, 3 to 4 minutes. Rinse under cold water. Drain well and divide the noodles among 4 large bowls.

- While the water for the noodles is heating, add 3 quarts water and the dried anchovies to a separate pot and bring to a boil. Reduce the heat and simmer for 5 to 7 minutes. Turn off the heat and remove the anchovies with a slotted spoon or mesh scoop and discard. Add the soy sauce to the water and return to a simmer.

- Mix the kimchi, sugar, and sesame oil together in a small bowl. Set aside.

- Heat the vegetable oil in a medium skillet over medium-high heat. Add the onion and sauté until translucent, 5 to 7 minutes.

- Divide the kimchi and onion among the 4 bowls of noodles.

- Just before serving, divide the hot broth among the bowls and serve immediately with Seasoned Soy Sauce.

MAKES 4 SERVINGS

Salt

1 pound dried somen noodles (about 4 bundles)

3 quarts water

½ cup dried anchovies *(myeolchi)*

¼ cup soy sauce

1 cup napa cabbage *(baechu)* kimchi, coarsely chopped, drained

1 teaspoon sugar

2 teaspoons Asian sesame oil

1 tablespoon vegetable oil

1 onion, thinly sliced

Seasoned Soy Sauce (page 155)

sweets and drinks

TRADITIONAL KOREAN MEALS AREN'T SERVED IN COURSES BUT rather laid out all at once. Still, that doesn't mean there aren't any delectables to satisfy your sweet tooth. Koreans have long enjoyed rice cakes and other sweets for snacks and special occasions.

A variety of hot and chilled beverages are also a staple of Korean cuisine. In addition to tea (green and otherwise), there are dozens of special drinks made from everything from native citrus *(yuja)* to Korean plums *(maeshil)*. There are also centuries-old traditions that go along with the drinking of tea and its rituals. Some of them are so formal that they seem odd to our modern sensibilities.

Today there are hundreds of small tea shops in Korea where you can take a break from everyday life and slow down for a lovely drink.

I've included updated versions of traditional favorites such as the Watermelon Punch (page 149) and Chilled Cinnamon-Ginger Tea (page 147), which make for lovely after-dinner beverages or even a nice group beverage for parties. I've also included some new *soju* cocktails and a couple of recipes that make wonderful desserts for even the fanciest of meals.

poached asian pear

(baesook)

An updated version of a traditional Korean sweet, this is one of my favorite ways to top off a meal. If you want, you can serve the slices of pear with a small scoop of vanilla ice cream and a lovely cup of Hot Ginger Tea (page 150) or green tea. Asian pears are in season in late autumn.

MAKES 4 SERVINGS

10 cups water
One 1-inch piece ginger, thinly sliced
2 or 3 strips lemon zest
1 large Asian pear, or 2 smaller ones
1 tablespoon whole black peppercorns
5 or 6 whole cloves
1 tablespoon sugar

- Pour the water into a large saucepan and add the ginger. Twist the strips of lemon zest and drop them in the water. Simmer over low heat for about 30 minutes, then strain, discarding the ginger and lemon zest.

- In the meantime, peel and core the pear, then cut it into ½-inch-thick slices. Add the pear, peppercorns, cloves, and sugar to the liquid and bring to a boil. Reduce the heat and simmer until the pear turns soft, about 15 minutes. Remove from the heat.

- Spoon out the pear slices and serve warm, at room temperature, or chilled, arranged in individual dessert bowls.

sweet spiced rice
(yakbap or yakshik)

This is a simplified version of a more complicated rice dish made for special occasions. It's a fragrant and delicious way to enjoy sticky rice. Although fresh chestnuts make their way into markets in the autumn, you can now find peeled chestnuts in the frozen section of most Korean markets all year. Jujubes can be found in the dried goods section of Korean and Chinese groceries.

⚙ Cover the rice with water and soak for about 4 hours, then drain. Line a steamer with a wet cotton cloth, add the rice, cover and steam for 30 minutes over boiling water.

⚙ In the meantime, cut the chestnuts and jujubes into quarters.

⚙ Carefully transfer the rice to a large bowl (it's still very hot!). Add the chestnuts, jujubes, brown sugar, soy sauce, cinnamon, sesame oil, and honey and toss to mix. Return the whole thing to the steamer and let steam for another 30 minutes.

⚙ Spoon the rice mixture into 4 individual bowls and sprinkle generously with pine nuts. Serve warm or at room temperature.

MAKES 4 TO 6 SERVINGS

2 cups sticky (glutinous) rice
5 chestnuts, peeled
5 jujubes/dried red dates *(daechu),* pitted
¾ cup (packed) dark brown sugar
2 teaspoons soy sauce
1 tablespoon ground cinnamon
1 tablespoon Asian sesame oil
1 tablespoon honey
Pine nuts for garnish

chilled cinnamon-ginger tea

(soojong gwa)

Although this is a chilled beverage, it is traditionally enjoyed in the winter. The "fire" of the cinnamon and ginger is supposed to warm you up, while the coolness of the beverage balances the heat. Not being much of a traditionalist, I like to make it during the summer and keep pitchers of it available as an alternative to iced tea.

- Pour the water into a large pot. Add the cinnamon and ginger and bring to a boil. Reduce the heat and simmer for about 30 minutes.

- Remove from the heat and carefully remove the cinnamon and ginger. Add the brown sugar and stir until completely dissolved. Let cool, then refrigerate for several hours (preferably overnight) until chilled.

- If you wish, sprinkle a few pine nuts in each cup before serving.

MAKES 15 TO 20 SERVINGS

1 gallon water
3 sticks cinnamon
One 2- to 3-inch piece ginger, sliced
¼ cup (packed) brown sugar
Pine nuts for garnish (optional)

watermelon punch

(soobak hwachae)

Great for a summertime picnic, a backyard party, or just to cool off the family after a hot day. If you want to be fancy, you can cut the edges of the hollowed-out watermelon into zigzags (be careful with the knife!). It's best to use a watermelon that's been chilled in the refrigerator, but you can just add extra ice if you didn't plan ahead.

MAKES ABOUT 20 SERVINGS

- Cut the watermelon about one-third from the top and trim a little bit off the bottom to make it sit flat.

- Have a large bowl ready and scoop out the insides with a melon baller or small spoon. Scrape out the remaining watermelon and reserve in a separate bowl. Using a piece of cheesecloth, squeeze out the juice from the remaining watermelon into the bowl with the watermelon balls.

- Add the sugar and lemon juice and stir until the sugar is dissolved. Add ice and let cool for a few minutes.

- When you're ready to serve, transfer the punch to the watermelon bowl, add more ice, and garnish with pine nuts if you wish.

1 small seedless watermelon
   (about 10 pounds)
½ cup sugar
Juice of 1 lemon
Lots of ice cubes
Pine nuts for garnish (optional)

VARIATIONS:
If you want, you can add other fruits to the punch. Good options are cantaloupe, honeydew melon, strawberries, pineapple, mandarin oranges, lychee, or Asian pears.

NOTE:
Traditional hwachae *is made with sugar syrup, which can be made by mixing equal amounts of sugar and water and heating the mixture over low heat until the sugar is completely dissolved. Let it cool completely before adding. Sugar syrup is great for iced tea, lemonade, or any number of chilled drinks.*

hot ginger tea

(saeng-gang cha)

Nothing warms you up like a hot cup of ginger tea. The warmth of the liquid and the spiciness don't just taste great on a winter day, but ginger also helps warm up your hands and feet since it increases blood circulation. This spicy-sweet tea is supposed to be good for your digestion, too.

- Add the ginger and water to a small pot and bring to a boil. Reduce the heat and simmer for about 10 minutes. Discard the ginger.

- Serve steaming hot, sprinkled with a few pine nuts if you wish. Provide some honey or sugar to sweeten to taste.

MAKES 2 SERVINGS

One 1-inch piece ginger, sliced
3 cups water
Pine nuts for garnish (optional)
Honey or sugar

soju cocktails

A distilled liquor made from potato, sweet potatoes, or yams, *soju* is historically the commoner's drink in Korea. Many hip and happening joints have been serving *soju* beverages, not only because it's a clean-tasting alcohol that's easy to use for mixed drinks, but also because its relatively low alcohol content helps get around liquor laws in certain cities. Here are a few fun cocktails with an Asian twist.

---

lemon-ginger martini

The lemon is traditional, but the ginger adds an element of surprise. Use a vegetable peeler to make a long strip of lemon zest for garnish. To rim your glasses with sugar, rub the rim with a wedge of lemon, then dip the glass upside down in a plate of sugar.

Squeeze the lemon juice into a cocktail shaker. Add the *soju*, ginger, sugar, and fill the shaker with ice cubes and shake vigorously. Strain into two sugar-rimmed cocktail glasses. Garnish with strips of lemon zest, lemon wedges, sprigs of mint, or whatever you like.

MAKES 2 COCKTAILS

½ lemon
3 ounces *soju*
One 1-inch piece ginger, sliced
2 tablespoons sugar
Ice cubes

watermelon chiller

This refreshing cocktail is perfect for those hot summer days. If you don't have time to freeze the watermelon beforehand, just add some ice cubes before blending.

🍸 Put the watermelon cubes in the freezer and freeze for an hour or two.

🍸 Put the watermelon, *soju*, lime juice, and sugar in a blender and blend until there are no chunks of ice left and it's well blended. Pour into 3 or 4 cocktail glasses. Garnish with a slice of watermelon, a wedge of lime, or whatever you like.

MAKES 3 OR 4 COCKTAILS

2 cups watermelon cubes, seeded
½ cup *soju*
Juice of 1 lime
1 tablespoon sugar

apple-pear cocktail

This is a nice beverage to serve at a dinner party in the fall when both apples and pears are in season.

🍸 Peel and core the apple and pear and cut into thin strips. Put the fruit in a pitcher and pour in the *soju*. Cover and refrigerate for at least 30 minutes or up to 2 hours.

🍸 Fill 12 cocktail glasses with ice. Strain the *soju* into the glasses, dividing equally among them (about ¼ cup in each glass). Add a couple of apple and pear pieces to each glass and top off each drink with tonic water. Garnish with wedges of lime.

MAKES 12 COCKTAILS

1 Fuji apple
1 small Asian pear
3 cups *soju*
1 quart tonic water, chilled

cranberry delight

An elegant drink any time of year, the mint adds a refreshing edge to this sweet and tart beverage.

- Muddle the lime, sugar, and mint leaves together in a cocktail shaker. Fill the shaker with ice cubes, then add the *soju* and cranberry juice. Shake vigorously.

- Put a few cubes of ice into 2 cocktail glasses. Pour the drink into the glasses and garnish with wedges of lime or mint sprigs.

MAKES 2 COCKTAILS

1 lime, cut into wedges
2 tablespoons sugar
12 mint leaves
Ice cubes
½ cup *soju*
1½ cups cranberry juice

sauces and other basics

seasoned soy sauce

(yangnyeom ganjang)

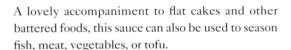

A lovely accompaniment to flat cakes and other battered foods, this sauce can also be used to season fish, meat, vegetables, or tofu.

MAKES ABOUT ½ CUP

¼ cup soy sauce
1 green onion, chopped
2 cloves garlic, minced
1 tablespoon Asian sesame oil
1 tablespoon toasted sesame seeds
1 teaspoon Korean chile powder
½ teaspoon freshly ground black pepper (optional)

↻ Combine the soy sauce, green onion, garlic, sesame oil, sesame seeds, chile powder, and black pepper (if using) in a small bowl.

↻ If serving as a dipping sauce, divide among small individual bowls. Leftovers can be stored in the refrigerator in a tightly sealed container for about 1 week.

vinegar soy sauce

(cho ganjang)

This serves as an especially good dipping sauce for deep-fried foods and dumplings.

MAKES ABOUT ½ CUP

¼ cup soy sauce
¼ cup white or rice vinegar
1 teaspoon Korean chile powder (optional)

↻ Combine the soy sauce, vinegar, and chile powder (if using) in a small bowl.

↻ If serving as a dipping sauce, divide among small individual bowls. Store leftovers in a tightly sealed container for about 1 week.

vinegar chile sauce

(cho gochujang)

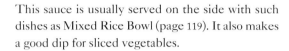

This spicy sauce is great for dipping sliced vegetables, such as cucumbers, peppers, and carrots, or to serve on the side with sashimi. (Koreans prefer this sauce to the Japanese soy-wasabi combination.) It is also good with Spicy Sashimi Rice (page 123).

MAKES ABOUT 4 SERVINGS

4 tablespoons Korean chile paste *(gochujang)*
4 tablespoons white, cider, or rice vinegar
2 tablespoons soy sauce
2 tablespoons sugar
2 tablespoons toasted sesame seeds
2 cloves garlic, minced
1 tablespoon Asian sesame oil

- Combine all the ingredients in a small bowl. It will keep in a tightly sealed container in the refrigerator for about 1 week.

seasoned chile paste

(yangnyeom gochujang)

This sauce is usually served on the side with such dishes as Mixed Rice Bowl (page 119). It also makes a good dip for sliced vegetables.

MAKES ABOUT ½ CUP

4 tablespoons Korean chile paste *(gochujang)*
2 tablespoons Asian sesame oil
1 tablespoon soy sauce
2 cloves garlic, minced
1 tablespoon toasted sesame seeds
1 tablespoon sugar or Korean malt syrup *(mool yut)*
1 green onion, chopped

- Combine all the ingredients in a small bowl. It will keep in a tightly sealed container in the refrigerator for about 1 week.

spicy soybean paste

(ssam dwenjang)

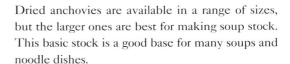

This is usually served with grilled meats and leaves of curly leaf lettuce or perilla leaves for wrapping. It also makes a good dip for sliced cucumbers, carrots, or Korean green chiles.

MAKES A SCANT 1 CUP

½ cup fermented soybean paste *(dwenjang)*
⅓ cup Korean chile paste *(gochujang)*
2 cloves garlic, minced
1 tablespoon Asian sesame oil
2 tablespoons rice wine
1 green bell pepper, minced (optional)

Stir the soybean paste, chile paste, garlic, sesame oil, rice wine, and bell pepper (if using) together in a small bowl until well mixed.

anchovy stock

(myeolchi gookmool)

Dried anchovies are available in a range of sizes, but the larger ones are best for making soup stock. This basic stock is a good base for many soups and noodle dishes.

MAKES ABOUT 2½ QUARTS

½ cup dried anchovies *(myeolchi)*
3 quarts (12 cups) water

Put the anchovies and water in a large pot. Bring to a boil, then reduce the heat and simmer for 5 to 7 minutes. Strain and discard the anchovies.

VARIATIONS:
You can also add a 2- to 3-inch piece of dashima *(kelp/seaweed) if you happen to have some on hand. To make a vegetarian broth, substitute dried shiitake mushrooms for the anchovies and simmer for an additional 5 to 7 minutes.*

quick & easy korean menus

TUMMY WARMER BREAKFAST
Black Sesame Porridge (page 39)
Hot Ginger Tea (page 150)

BACKYARD BARBECUE
Chicken Skewers with Green Onions (page 75)
Barbecued Beef Ribs (page 79)
Barbecued Pork Ribs (page 82)
Grilled Shrimp (page 93)
Seasoned Green Onion Salad (page 70)
Watermelon Punch (page 149)

CURE THE WINTER BLUES
Dumpling Soup with Rice Cakes (page 51)
Quick Kimchi (page 107)

AFTER-SCHOOL SNACK
Rice Cake Stick Snack (page 33)
Deep-Fried Kelp (page 68)
Chilled Cinnamon-Ginger Tea (page 147)

COMPLETELY VEGETARIAN
Green Onion Pancakes (page 34)
Seasoned Tofu (page 61)
Seasoned Spinach (page 63)
Sautéed Eggplant (page 65)
Bean Sprout Soup (page 55)
White rice

DOWN-HOME COUNTRY COOKING
Kimchi Hot Pot (page 53)
Soy Stewed Beef (page 87)
Daikon Kimchi (page 108)
White rice

KIDS' FAVORITES
Curry Rice (page 124) or Black Bean Noodles (page 134)
Seaweed Soup (page 52)
Deep-Fried Squid (page 40)

PACK-AWAY PICNIC
Seasoned Fried Chicken (page 78)
Seaweed Rice Rolls (page 125)
Korean Leek Pancakes (page 35)

ELEGANT DINNER PARTY
One of the *Soju* Cocktails (pages 151 to 153)
Skewered Beef (page 81)
Spicy Sashimi Rice (page 123)
Poached Asian Pear (page 145)

SPICE-LOVER'S SPECIAL (OR TURN UP THE HEAT)
Kimchi Pancakes (page 37)
Killer Spicy Mixed Noodles (page 138) or
Spicy Buckwheat Noodles (page 135)
Hot Ginger Tea (page 150)

mail-order sources for korean ingredients

ASIAN FOOD GROCER
131 West Harris Avenue
South San Francisco, CA 94080
888.482.2742
650.873.7600 x107
www.asianfoodgrocer.com
They have a decent selection of some dried goods but don't carry other necessities such as chile paste.

CHONG'S GROCERY
3560 W. 8th Street
Los Angeles, CA 90005
213.387.0651
A small family-owned business that makes the best sesame oil. They also carry sesame seeds and other dried goods.

IKOREAPLAZA.COM
2370 Telegraph Avenue
Oakland, CA 94617
510.238.8940
www.ikoreaplaza.com

PACIFIC RIM GOURMET
www.pacificrimgourmet.com
More of a general Asian ingredient provider with some, but not many, Korean items available.

KGROCER.COM
923 E. 3rd Street, Suite 115
Los Angeles, CA 90013
www.kgrocer.com
A great source for all kinds of dry goods, noodles, and even Korean DVDs.

books and resources on
foods, cooking, and culture of korea

Bartell, Karen Hulene. *The Best of Korean Cuisine*. New York, New York: Hippocrene Books, 2002.

Choe, Ji Sook, and Moriyama, Yukiko. *Quick and Easy Korean Cooking for Everyone*. Japan: Japan Publications Trading, 2003.

Choi, Young Sook. *Korean Cuisine*. Monterey Park, California: Wei-Chuan Publishing, 2001.

Chun, Injoo, et. al. *Authentic Recipes from Korea*. Berkeley, California: Periplus Editions, 2005.

Chung, Okwha, and Monroe, Judy. *Cooking the Korean Way: Revised and Expanded to Include New Low-Fat and Vegetarian Recipes*. Minneapolis, Minnesota: Lerner Publishing Group, 2002.

Chung, Soo-Yung. *Korean Home Cooking*. Berkeley, California: Tuttle Publishing, 2001.

Hepinstall, Hisoo Shin. *Growing Up in a Korean Kitchen: A Cookbook*. Berkeley, California: Ten Speed Press, 2001.

Hong, Kyeong-hee, and Brother Anthony of Taize. *The Korean Way of Tea*. Seoul, Korea: Seoul Selections, 2007.

Kim, Man-Jo, et. al. *The Kimchee Cookbook: Fiery Flavors and Cultural History of Korea's National Dish*. Berkeley, California: Periplus Editions, 1999.

Kwak, Jenny. *Dok Suni: Recipes from My Mother's Korean Kitchen*. New York, New York: St. Martin's Press, 1998.

Lee, Cecilia Hae-Jin. *Eating Korean: From Barbecue to Kimchi, Recipes from My Home*. New York, New York: Wiley, 2005.

Lee, Cecilia Hae-Jin. *Frommer's South Korea (Complete Guide)*. Hoboken, New Jersey: Wiley, 2008.

Marks, Copeland. *The Korean Kitchen: Classic Recipes from the Land of the Morning Calm*. San Francisco, California: Chronicle Books, 1999.

Park, Allisa. *Discovering Korean Cuisine: Recipes from the Best Korean Restaurants in Los Angeles*. Lomita, California: Dream Character, Inc., 2007.

Pettid, Michael J. *Korean Cuisine: An Illustrated History*. London, United Kingdom: Reaktion Books, 2008.

index

---

table of equivalents

The exact equivalents in the following tables have been rounded for convenience.

LIQUID/DRY MEASUREMENTS

U.S.	Metric
¼ teaspoon	1.25 milliliters
½ teaspoon	2.5 milliliters
1 teaspoon	5 milliliters
1 tablespoon	15 milliliters
1 fluid ounce (2 tablespoons)	30 milliliters
¼ cup	60 milliliters
⅓ cup	80 milliliters
½ cup	120 milliliters
1 cup	240 milliliters
1 pint (2 cups)	480 milliliters
1 quart (4 cups, 32 ounces)	960 milliliters
1 gallon (4 quarts)	3.84 liters
1 ounce (by weight)	28 grams
1 pound	448 grams
2.2 pounds	1 kilogram

LENGTHS

U.S.	Metric
⅛ inch	3 millimeters
¼ inch	6 millimeters
½ inch	12 millimeters
1 inch	2.5 centimeters

OVEN TEMPERATURE

Fahrenheit	Celsius	Gas
250	120	½
275	140	1
300	150	2
325	160	3
350	180	4
375	190	5
400	200	6
425	220	7
450	230	8
475	240	9
500	260	10